# MACMILLAN MASTER GUIDES

...LEGE

**MASTER GUIDES**

GENERAL EDITOR: JAMES GIBSON

| | |
|---|---|
| JANE AUSTEN | *Emma* Norman Page |
| | *Sense and Sensibility* Judy Simons |
| | *Persuasion* Judy Simons |
| | *Pride and Prejudice* Raymond Wilson |
| | *Mansfield Park* Richard Wirdnam |
| SAMUEL BECKETT | *Waiting for Godot* Jennifer Birkett |
| WILLIAM BLAKE | *Songs of Innocence and Songs of Experience* Alan Tomlinson |
| ROBERT BOLT | *A Man for All Seasons* Leonard Smith |
| CHARLOTTE BRONTË | *Jane Eyre* Robert Miles |
| EMILY BRONTË | *Wuthering Heights* Hilda D. Spear |
| JOHN BUNYAN | *The Pilgrim's Progress* Beatrice Batson |
| GEOFFREY CHAUCER | *The Miller's Tale* Michael Alexander |
| | *The Pardoner's Tale* Geoffrey Lester |
| | *The Wife of Bath's Tale* Nicholas Marsh |
| | *The Knight's Tale* Anne Samson |
| | *The Prologue to the Canterbury Tales* Nigel Thomas and Richard Swan |
| JOSEPH CONRAD | *The Secret Agent* Andrew Mayne |
| CHARLES DICKENS | *Bleak House* Dennis Butts |
| | *Great Expectations* Dennis Butts |
| | *Hard Times* Norman Page |
| GEORGE ELIOT | *Middlemarch* Graham Handley |
| | *Silas Marner* Graham Handley |
| | *The Mill on the Floss* Helen Wheeler |
| T. S. ELIOT | *Murder in the Cathedral* Paul Lapworth |
| | *Selected Poems* Andrew Swarbrick |
| HENRY FIELDING | *Joseph Andrews* Trevor Johnson |
| E. M. FORSTER | *A Passage to India* Hilda D. Spear |
| | *Howards End* Ian Milligan |
| WILLIAM GOLDING | *The Spire* Rosemary Sumner |
| | *Lord of the Flies* Raymond Wilson |
| OLIVER GOLDSMITH | *She Stoops to Conquer* Paul Ranger |
| THOMAS HARDY | *The Mayor of Casterbridge* Ray Evans |
| | *Tess of the d'Urbervilles* James Gibson |
| | *Far from the Madding Crowd* Colin Temblett-Wood |
| BEN JONSON | *Volpone* Michael Stout |
| JOHN KEATS | *Selected Poems* John Garrett |
| RUDYARD KIPLING | *Kim* Leonée Ormond |
| PHILIP LARKIN | *The Less Deceived* and Andrew Swarbrick |

# MACMILLAN MASTER GUIDES

| | |
|---|---|
| D.H. LAWRENCE | *Sons and Lovers* R. P. Draper |
| HARPER LEE | *To Kill a Mockingbird* Jean Armstrong |
| LAURIE LEE | *Cider with Rosie* Brian Tarbitt |
| GERARD MANLEY HOPKINS | *Selected Poems* R. J. C. Watt |
| CHRISTOPHER MARLOWE | *Doctor Faustus* David A. Male |
| THE METAPHYSICAL POETS | Joan van Emden |
| THOMAS MIDDLETON and WILLIAM ROWLEY | *The Changeling* Tony Bromham |
| ARTHUR MILLER | *The Crucible* Leonard Smith<br>*Death of a Salesman* Peter Spalding |
| GEORGE ORWELL | *Animal Farm* Jean Armstrong |
| WILLIAM SHAKESPEARE | *Richard II* Charles Barber<br>*Othello* Tony Bromham<br>*Hamlet* Jean Brooks<br>*King Lear* Francis Casey<br>*Henry V* Peter Davison<br>*The Winter's Tale* Diana Devlin<br>*Julius Caesar* David Elloway<br>*Macbeth* David Elloway<br>*The Merchant of Venice* A. M. Kinghorn<br>*Measure for Measure* Mark Lilly<br>*Henry IV Part I* Helen Morris<br>*Romeo and Juliet* Helen Morris<br>*A Midsummer Night's Dream* Kenneth Pickering<br>*The Tempest* Kenneth Pickering<br>*Coriolanus* Gordon Williams<br>*Antony and Cleopatra* Martin Wine<br>*Twelfth Night* R. P. Draper |
| GEORGE BERNARD SHAW | *St Joan* Leonée Ormond |
| RICHARD SHERIDAN | *The School for Scandal* Paul Ranger<br>*The Rivals* Jeremy Rowe |
| ALFRED TENNYSON | *In Memoriam* Richard Gill |
| EDWARD THOMAS | *Selected Poems* Gerald Roberts |
| ANTHONY TROLLOPE | *Barchester Towers* K. M. Newton |
| JOHN WEBSTER | *The White Devil* and *The Duchess of Malfi* David A. Male |
| VIRGINIA WOOLF | *To the Lighthouse* John Mepham<br>*Mrs Dalloway* Julian Pattison |
| WILLIAM WORDSWORTH | *The Prelude Books I and II* Helen Wheeler |

# MACMILLAN MASTER GUIDES

# TO KILL A MOCKINGBIRD

# BY HARPER LEE

## JEAN ARMSTRONG

**M**

MACMILLAN

First published 1987 by
THE MACMILLAN PRESS LTD
Houndmills, Basingstoke, Hampshire RG21 2XS
and London
Companies and representatives
throughout the world

ISBN 0–333–39854–8

A catalogue record for this book is available
from the British Library.

Reprinted 1989, 1990, 1992, 1993, 1994


Printed in China

# CONTENTS

# GENERAL EDITOR'S PREFACE

The aim of the Macmillan Master Guides is to help you to appreciate the book you are studying by providing information about it and by suggesting ways of reading and thinking about it which will lead to a fuller understanding. The sections on the writer's life and background have been designed to illustrate those aspects of the writer's life which have influenced the work, and to place it in its personal and literary context. The summaries and critical commentary are of special importance in that each brief summary of the action is followed by an examination of the significant critical points. The space which might have been given to repetitive explanatory notes has been devoted to a detailed analysis of the kind of passage which might confront you in an examination. Literary criticism is concerned with both the broader aspects of the work being studied and with its detail. The ideas which meet us in reading a great work of literature, and their relevance to us today, are an essential part of our study, and our Guides look at the thought of their subject in some detail. But just as essential is the craft with which the writer has constructed his work of art, and this may be considered under several technical headings − characterisation, language, style and stagecraft, for example.

The authors of these Guides are all teachers and writers of wide experience, and they have chosen to write about books they admire and know well in the belief that they can communicate their admiration to you. But you yourself must read and know intimately the book you are studying. No one can do that for you. You should see this book as a lamp-post. Use it to shed light, not to lean against. If you know your text and know what it is saying about life, and how it says it, then you will enjoy it, and there is no better way of passing an examination in literature.

JAMES GIBSON

# Acknowledgement

Cover illustration: *Summer Evening, Hook End Farm* by Gilbert Spencer. Photograph © City of Bristol Museum and Art Gallery, by courtesy of the Bridgeman Art Library.

# 1 THE AUTHOR AND THE BACKGROUND TO THE NOVEL

Nelle Harper Lee was born on 26 April 1926 in Monroeville, Alabama, which is most certainly the Maycomb of the novel. She was the youngest daughter of a lawyer and began to write early in childhood while she was attending local schools. Her satirical presentation of education in the novel suggests that she found much to criticise there.

Harper Lee studied law at the State University of Alabama at Tuscaloosa, spending a year as an exchange student at Oxford University, but left six months before the final exams to settle in New York. Here she worked for a time as an airline reservations clerk. Encouraged by an agent to whom she sent her work, she gave up her job to write full time and after substantial revision, *To Kill a Mockingbird* was published in 1960, three years after its first submission to a publisher. It was immediately acclaimed and became a bestseller, translated into many languages. The novel won three literary awards, one of which was the coveted Pulitzer Prize in 1961. Other winners of this important prize have been John Steinbeck (1940), Ernest Hemingway (1953) and William Faulkner (1955).

Harper Lee lives in New York and since the 1950s has been a full-time writer, contributing to *Vogue* and other journals, but has published no other novel. Another is promised, again about small-town Southern life, that 'last refuge of eccentrics'. The novelist Jane Austen, she believes, has been her greatest literary influence.

*To Kill a Mockingbird* is firmly in the tradition of Southern literature and of such authors as William Faulkner and Carson McCullers. Scout, the heroine, has been compared to Frankie in McCullers' *The Member of the Wedding* (1946). This tradition, with its deep sense of tragedy, may be the result of the South's defeat in the American Civil War (1861–5). Here the issue of slavery finally split the Northern and the Southern States which until then had maintained an uneasy bond. The agricultural structure of the Southern communities depended upon black slaves but the Northern States were industrialised, and Northerners came to feel more and more that they could not condone the existence of slavery in the South. The matter came to a head in 1861 when the Southern States broke away from the American Union and joined together as the Confederate States of America. War was declared and fighting continued for four years until General Robert E. Lee surrendered the Confederate Army in 1865.

This defeat by the Northerners may have strengthened the identity of the Southern States, however, and reinforced their loyalties to Southern values and traditions, bringing them closer together. Their attitudes certainly hardened and the slaves were free in name only. Whites at the bottom of the social ladder felt threatened by the negroes' new place in society and wanted to protect their own position. The Southern States resisted the influence and the imposition of Northern values during the reconstruction period after the Civil War, and they did everything possible to preserve white supremacy. But the old, leisured, aristocratic life-style had gone.

Southern novels tend to be regional and convey a strong sense of place, but they also convey a sense of loneliness, of isolation. The Southern States were cut off from the progressive North and suffered many years of decline, especially as the agricultural communities were hardest hit by the depression. Many Southerners moved North where there were better opportunities for education and for work, but they then felt cut off from the place where they had spent their childhood and the traditions in which they had been raised. This resulted in a feeling of exile and nostalgia. Those who moved often suffered from mixed feelings: they were dismayed to see the break-up of the old communities and traditions, but hated the Southern values which had driven them north in the first place. This ambivalence is evident in Southern literature and in *To Kill a Mockingbird*, where the town of Maycomb is presented both critically and nostalgically.

The pain of isolation is poignantly presented in the characters of Boo Radley and Mayella Ewell, both of whom make a desperate attempt at human contact. Both have been made victims through the unyielding prejudices of society. Dolphus Raymond, a rich landowner, is also isolated from the white community as he lives with a negro woman and has half-caste children whom he sends north. We see here how the values of the North are perceived to be quite different, and the difference between Northern and Southern values is evident throughout the novel. In a community so cut off from any but its own prejudices, those who do not fit, those who think or act in a way which is considered to be out of line, suffer the pain of isolation as a consequence. In Southern communities there is no room for those who do not conform.

Southern novels are also characterised by a sense of guilt. While white Southerners are proud of their aristocratic heritage – and this is evident in *To Kill a Mockingbird* where different notions of 'Fine-Folk' are discussed – they also carry a burden of guilt about their attitude to slavery. Racial tension is obviously present, for while abolition forced Southerners to free their slaves, their attitudes were slow to change. The central theme of the novel, the wrongful conviction of an innocent negro, was by no means unusual. *The Times* of October 1976 published an account of an Alabama negro's wrongful conviction for rape in 1931, and his eventual pardon 45 years later.

Another characteristic of the Southern novel is violence. Southern values contribute to this as honour must be defended at all costs, even – as we see in the novel – if you are a Ewell and live on the rubbish dump. Much of the violence was inevitably directed towards the negroes who were seen to be, at best, children needing firm handling, and at worst, as ineducable, immoral people not to be trusted especially where women were concerned. They were rumoured to have great sexual prowess, an attribute which led to many charges of rape and subsequent lynchings. The Sarum men coming in the night for Tom Robinson are firmly in this tradition. The fear of losing 'face' and 'place' was strengthened by the granting of free status to negroes and is a strong element in Southern literature. Much of the violence is the result of this fear.

Southerners not only prided themselves on their traditional culture but also on the particular 'manliness' of their men and the 'femininity' of their women. The Southern man was traditionally courageous in a swashbuckling, reckless way, quick-tempered and quick to take offence; he had a low regard for human life. The women were expected to be fragile creatures, pure and in need of protection. The strong influence of this sexual stereotyping is evident in *To Kill a Mockingbird* and reaches its climax in Mayella's retort to the judge and jury at the close of her evidence. This is an appeal no traditional Southern gentleman could resist, but it is not only Atticus who resists it – refusing to uphold the 'fiction' that Mayella could not possibly have made sexual advances to a negro – but also one of the Cunninghams. Mr Cunningham was one of the Sarum crowd who was ready, not long before, to continue the old lynching tradition, so we can see Harper Lee's optimism in this respect. If the Cunninghams can change their position and shed their prejudices, there is much to hope for.

While this novel realises all the traditional tragic elements of Southern fiction and depicts all the old, backward attitudes, it also moves forward into a future that sees the South relinquishing these slowly, without necessarily losing its sense of community and its separate identity. After rebelling for so long against being a girl and all that this implies in a Southern State, Scout eventually comes to see that being a 'lady' demands courage and dignity and can be as remote from the Missionary Society model of Southern womanhood as Atticus' version of a Southern gentleman is from the trigger-happy, bigoted but essentially traditional Nathan Radley.

# 2 SUMMARIES AND CRITICAL COMMENTARY

## PART I

### Chapter 1

*Summary*

We are introduced to Scout's family and their origins. The Finches have lived on the homestead known as Finch's Landing for generations until Atticus Finch, Scout's father, broke the tradition of living off the land by leaving for Montgomery to study law. His sister Alexandra remained to continue the family tradition but his brother, John Hale (Uncle Jack), took up medicine when Atticus began his practice in Maycomb, a town twenty miles east of the Landing, and was able to assist him financially.

Scout (Jean Louise) has an elder brother Jem (Jeremy) who is introduced to us as a keen footballer with an injured arm. Scout's narrative will recount the events which culminate in this injury and it begins when she is almost six and Jem almost ten. Involved in these events is Dill (Charles Baker Harris), the nephew of Miss Rachel Haverford (Aunt Rachel), next-door-neighbour of the Finches. We also meet Calpurnia, the Finch family's cook and the children's mother-substitute, for their mother died when Scout was born. Calpurnia is a negress and is much loved and respected by the Finch family.

Dill comes to spend the summer holidays with his aunt and the children play dramatic games together, influenced by books and films, and finally, by an enigmatic character Boo (Arthur) Radley who is a neighbour of the Finches, and about whom there are many rumours. Boo never leaves home except at night. Dill is fascinated and wants to entice Boo out of his house to see what he is really like.

*Commentary*
The story is narrated in retrospect which allows the author to retain many of the advantages of having a child narrator while losing many of the disadvantages. A child's language is too restrictive and a child's experience and understanding too simple for a novel of depth and scope, but many opportunities for humour can be exploited and moral issues can be presented with simple clarity. By having the adult Scout recount the story from the distance of some years, and with a more mature understanding of the events, freshness of the child's experience is retained without its restrictions.

Historical facts help to present a society built upon prejudice and injustice and it is against this background, resistant to change and development, that Atticus is seen as one of the forward-looking people. President Roosevelt's maxim that the people had 'nothing to fear but fear itself', introduces one of the major thrusts of the novel, for fear – of the unknown, of losing face and place in society, of change and development – is at the root of nearly all that is tragic in the novel, and its opposite, courage, is seen to be the antidote as a force that can slowly bring about the necessary movement towards a more civilised way of life. The children take their first clumsy step in this direction when Dill tells them of his impressions of Maycomb. The chapter ends with a physical and symbolic step into the future.

**Chapter 2**

*Summary*
Scout is miserable when Dill leaves Maycomb at the close of the school holidays, but she is cheered by the prospect of starting school. She is disappointed, however, for her teacher, Miss Caroline, is an advocate of progressive teaching methods and disapproves of her ability to read and write before attending school. A further misunderstanding takes place when Scout attempts to explain why Walter Cunningham, the child of country people, is unable to borrow money to buy himself lunch. Walter's condition and Atticus' explanation to Scout about the financial position of the farmers who are trying to hold on to their land, make clear that they were the hardest hit by the crash. Their poverty is such that, unable to pay cash, they have to pay for services in kind. Walter's father figures prominently later in the novel.

*Commentary*
Here we have an example of the candour of the child narrator used to good effect. Scout is puzzled by Miss Caroline's attitudes but we are aware of the ironic implications. Scout has never been taught to read

in any formal way yet, much to her teacher's chagrin she can do so adequately; she can write too but is told she must forget how to do so until the appropriate time! Here the author is not only poking fun at the progressive teaching practices of the time, but is laying one of the foundation stones of the novel by gently ridiculing a dogmatic approach which values a system rather than its objective. A further turn of the screw is Jem's humorous misunderstanding of what the Dewey Decimal System really is. It is a system for classifying books and is here used ironically to support the absurdity of Miss Caroline's rigid ideas, and her treatment of Scout as a member of a Grade rather than as an individual. If Maycomb was presented in Chapter 1 as slow-moving and backward, here the folly of a too-enthusiastic acceptance of what is new is humorously suggested.

## Chapter 3

*Summary*
When Jem meets Scout after morning school, he invites Walter home to lunch. Scout embarrasses Walter by commenting on the way he eats and is given a lesson in good manners by Calpurnia.

During afternoon school, Miss Caroline has to deal with filthy and foul-mouthed Burris Ewell. When a cootie crawls out of his hair Miss Caroline screams with horror but is soon enlightened about the nature and habits of the feckless Ewell family who live near the town's rubbish dump in absolute squalor. When Burris is told to go home and wash, he becomes abusive and insults Miss Caroline. His father, Bob Ewell, is one of the most important characters in the novel and Burris exhibits traits of character we are later to see displayed by his father.

Scout has not enjoyed her first day at school and when recounting the day's events to her father in the evening, she asks him why she has to go to school when the Ewells may stay at home. Atticus explains that for some people exceptions have to be made and Scout learns to compromise.

*Commentary*
Jem's character is developed further in this chapter when he invites Walter to lunch after reprimanding his sister for fighting with him. He is shown to have natural tact and by the time the children reach the Finches' house, Walter was completely at his ease. This tact was evident in Chapter 1 when Jem rescued Dill from Scout's embarrassing questions and it is a characteristic we find he has inherited or learnt from his father. Jem's courteous behaviour is contrasted with Scout's impulsiveness. Her excuse that Walter, as a

Cunningham, is not 'company' earns her only a further reproof from Calpurnia when she offers this as an explanation for her behaviour. The message in this episode seems to be that social position is of no consequence if the responsibilities which this confers are ignored. Jem's behaviour is set against the conventional Southern code towards women, demonstrated in this chapter by the boy's chivalry towards Miss Caroline.

We see his natural tact and sensitivity against a background of traditional behaviour which, at the moment, seems civil and reasonable but which is later to prove inadequate.

We will later appreciate the irony of Atticus' attitude towards the Ewells who are, to some extent, outside the law. Here he takes a lenient view of Bob Ewell's illegal activities but Ewell later demands full rigour against Tom Robinson whom he has falsely accused. The idea that a dogmatic, unyielding application of the law is contrary to a Christian way of life is being suggested here, and the novel presents, in different ways, the idea that laws and doctrines may do more harm than good if indiscriminately applied. The answer appears to be not in rules and regulations, codes and conventions, but in an imaginative leap towards understanding. 'You never really understand a person . . . until you climb into his skin', Atticus tells Scout, and this is part of the framework of the novel; within it the characters are judged by how well they are able to make this leap.

## Chapter 4

*Summary*
Scout resigns herself to boredom at school but the holidays soon return and Dill returns with them. She has discovered chewing gum in a knot-hole in one of the oaks near the Radley house but Jem orders her to spit it out in case it is poisoned. They later find old coins in the knot-hole and Jem realises that these are valuable. This makes him think more deeply about their finds.

With the return of Dill the children begin their dramatic games once more, but Jem has invented a new one based on rumour and neighbourhood legend, about Boo Radley. This game they call 'One Man's Family'. Atticus catches them playing this and suspects them of tormenting Boo, but Jem lies to him.

During one of the children's games with a tyre, Scout is rolled right up to the Radley house much to everybody's alarm, and though she does not tell the others, she is sure she has heard someone laughing at her from inside the house.

*Commentary*

There is further satire here on the educational methods of the time and Scout is bored and feels she is being cheated out of something.

The children structure their imaginative concept of Boo Radley and his life into a drama, but this is balanced in the chapter by the real events which have taken place in the development of their relationship with him. Although they are as yet unaware of it, except for Jem's suspicions, the gifts in the tree are Boo Radley's attempt to make real contact, and the laugh Scout heard suggests that, unknown to them, he is involved in their life as a spectator. The mysterious nature of Boo Radley is well sustained here and the suspense is heightened by the intermingling of the real and the imaginary.

The language too, continues to be a mixture of racy colloquialism and suggestive metaphor. This might be a suitable time to pause and consider the effect of figurative language in the novel as this should, by now, have become evident as an important part of the author's style. In Chapters 1 and 2 we have vivid descriptions of people in metaphors well suited to a child's view of the world. Miss Caroline 'looked and smelled like a peppermint drop' but Calpurnia has none of this sweet-smelling softness, being described as 'all angles and bones' while 'her hand was wide as a bed slat and twice as hard'. Through metaphors of this kind we not only see as Scout sees, but come to understand how she relates to different people in her life.

Vivid description of this kind is offset by the colloquial language of the children which has by now established itself as racy and authentic, giving the novel its realistic flavour, while Atticus' legalistic diction (Chapter 3) adds yet another dimension. The novel is characterised by a variety of language and the way the characters express themselves is indicative of their place in this highly-structured society. Calpurnia, for example, becomes ungrammatical when she is angry (Chapter 3) and as the novel develops, her speech alters in different circumstances. We have also met the country dialect of Walter Cunningham with his superstitious dread of the Radleys, and the abusive tone and turn of phrase which is a characteristic of the Ewells, a language which is defensive and offensive simultaneously.

## Chapter 5

*Summary*

Jem and Dill spend a lot of time together as the summer progresses and Scout seeks out the company of a neighbour, Miss Maudie Atkinson. Miss Maudie tells Scout something of Boo Radley's background, dismissing contemptuously the rumours about him which she refers to as gossip, attributing some to Stephanie Crawford who is one of the local white community and an inveterate gossip. The Radley house is a sad house, Scout learns, and in her account of the Radleys, we learn a great deal about the character of Miss Maudie herself.

The following day Scout is once again included in the boys' activities and joins them as they try to make Boo Radley come out of his house by delivering a letter on the end of a fishing rod. Atticus catches them red-handed and forbids them to annoy Boo in any way or to play the game 'One Man's Family'.

*Commentary*
The chapter is divided roughly into two. The first half develops the picture of the real Arthur Radley and the second begins the children's attempts to make contact with their fantasy figure.

Scout's conversation with Miss Maudie reinforces the picture of the Radley family presented in Chapter 1. They belong to a religious sect characterised by their humility, and ironically this causes the incarceration and eventual damage of Arthur (Boo). They are ready, too, to damn Miss Maudie for the time she spends in her garden among 'natural' things while unable to see how unnatural they have made life for their son, stunting him with their bigotry. Miss Maudie remembers Arthur as a boy who 'spoke as nicely as he knew how'; she hints at what goes on in families behind closed doors. Scout's defence of her father effects a contrast here and brings one of the themes of the novel – family life – to the fore, inviting a contrast between the Radleys and the Finches. Dill's family are also offered for comparison as Scout catches him out telling lies about his father again. He insists that all is well at home but we are beginning to suspect that this is not so.

We can again appreciate the advantages of the child narrator. Scout's sense of fair play and her limited understanding of what Miss Maudie is telling her, allow the author to exploit opportunities for humour and ironic comment as, for example, when Scout misunderstands about the whisky and leaps to the defence of her father.

## Chapter 6

*Summary*
It is Dill's last night in Maycomb and the children try to take a look inside the Radley house. Nathan Radley, Boo's elder brother, assumes the disturbance is caused by a negro intruder and shoots. The children make their escape but in doing so Jem becomes caught

on the fence and has to leave his trousers behind. A group of neighbours have gathered to see what the commotion is about and there is a humorous scene when Jem is seen without his trousers. Dill comes to his rescue by explaining that they were playing strip poker. Some of the neighbourhood attitudes are revealed in Scout's later comment. Jem returns later in the night to collect his trousers.

## Commentary

We continue to build up our picture of the Radley family from the description here, where we learn that the back of the house was 'less inviting than the front' which itself repelled rather than attracted visitors. Here at the back, no appearances are kept up, and this reinforces the idea of the Radleys as hypocrites and reminds us of Miss Maudie's comment about what goes on behind closed doors.

Dill's mental agility is evident and contrasts with the way Jem was out-manoeuvred by his father in the previous chapter, but here Jem realises that his father's point of view is right and they were wrong to interfere with Boo in the way they did. We see this episode has been a growing point for Jem especially, and his personal courage and respect for his father's standards move him into a new stage of maturity.

Notice the way the narrative is constructed here, moving from a humorous opening to taut suspense and acute observation through heightened perception in the darkness.

## Chapter 7

### Summary

Jem appears moody and eventually tells Scout that when he collected his trousers they had been mended. They find first twine and then soap sculptures of themselves in the tree hole where they had previously found the chewing gum and the Indian coins. Later still they find a spelling medal and then a pocket watch on a chain. Because the soap miniatures represent the two of them, they now view their finds as gifts left especially for them, and they decide to leave a thank-you note in the tree. They are unable to do so, however, because they find the hole has been filled with cement. Jem asks Mr Nathan Radley about this and is told he filled the hole because the tree was dying. When Jem checks this with Atticus he finds it to be untrue and his suspicion that the gifts are from Boo Radley is confirmed. Scout later notices that Jem has been crying.

*Commentary*

Jem's similarity to his father is evident in this chapter as he puts together his suspicions and the evidence that suggests Boo Radley has left the gifts for them. The dialogue in the chapter is a foretaste of the court scene to come, where facts and prejudices are carefully assessed to discover the truth. Jem's sensitivity is obvious in the way he is moved to tears by Boo's situation, but while he weeps for Boo he comforts his sister and protects her from what he has found so distressing. Nathan Radley's character is consolidated here. In the previous chapter his trigger-happy nature was evident and now we find it is not only intruders he wishes to discourage: he is prepared to cut off his brother absolutely from all friendly contact with the outside world, even with children.

## Chapter 8

*Summary*

Winter comes to Maycomb and old Mrs Radley dies. Scout experiences snow for the first time and the children build a snowman. During the night Miss Maudie's house catches fire and the neighbourhood turns out to fight it. Someone puts a blanket round Scout's shoulders and it turns out to be Boo Radley. Miss Maudie shows great strength of character when her house is burnt to the ground and we find it was her kind heart that caused the fire.

*Commentary*

This chapter develops much that has been introduced earlier. Jem's sensitivity is consolidated by the way he 'rescues' worms from the soil which he moves, and also by the way he wishes to prevent Boo suffering for his kindness to Scout. His ingenuity is seen in the way he manages to build a snowman with so little snow, which elicits from Atticus the remark, 'I'll never worry about what'll become of you son, you'll always have an idea.'

Mr Avery, whom we met humorously in Chapter 6, is seen to be another of the town's eccentric and prejudiced characters. However, despite the fact that he can be so easily caricatured and is presented as grotesque even when helping to fight the fire, he does so at considerable personal risk. Here is another example of a character who is something more than appearance suggests. His references to 'bad children' causing the snow and to Appomatox (the village where General Lee surrendered to Northern Forces during the Civil War), show his ingrained prejudice and how much the War dominated the imagination of these people.

Miss Maudie's attitude to the destruction of her home is an example of the courage the author wishes to present as a positive value. Many examples are evident in the novel and together they form one of the important themes, 'courage is not just a man with a gun in his hand'. This chapter prepares us for the development of this theme in Chapters 10 and 11.

## Chapter 9

*Summary*
Atticus explains to Scout why he must defend a negro accused of rape. This is the first reference to the story of Tom Robinson and Atticus' involvement in his trial. He tells Scout his conscience dictates he must defend Tom, even though he is aware he will not win his case as all the odds are against him. Scout has begun to feel the effects of her father's involvement as one of her schoolmates has taunted her because of Atticus' work for negroes. Atticus warns Scout about the possibility of such comments at school, but he advises her to resist provocation.

She attempts to follow this advice but, spending Christmas at Aunt Alexandra's, her cousin Francis provokes her to violence in the same way as Cecil Jacobs did earlier, by insulting Atticus for defending negroes. She is chastised by Uncle Jack for fighting and especially for the language she uses, but when he eventually hears her side of the story he apologises. Scout overhears Atticus telling Uncle Jack that he hopes the trial will not affect his children adversely, and that they will go to him for answers rather than listen to town gossip and be corrupted by it. Scout later realises that she was intended to overhear this conversation.

*Commentary*
The major theme of the novel, the evil of prejudice and especially of racial prejudice, has been introduced in the attitude of the people of Maycomb towards the negroes. They speak of them contemptuously as 'niggers', a term Atticus tells Scout not to use and which we notice Miss Maudie does not use. Negroes have been seen to be superstitious, they live in a settlement beyond the town dump and they do menial work. In contrast, we have met Calpurnia and come to respect her, in turn respecting her opinion of Tom Robinson whom Atticus is to defend. All Atticus has in Tom's defence is a 'black man's word', against which is balanced the whole history of negroes in the South, a disadvantage Atticus knows he cannot overcome. His courage is shown in his determination to persevere.

The prevailing attitude towards negroes is seen in the way no one finds anything amiss in Nathan Radley's action when he shoots at what he thinks is a negro in his cabbage patch (Chapter 6), and in Cecil

Jacob's remark. Atticus tells Uncle Jack that people go mad when anything to do with a negro comes up and he sees the town's racialism as a disease that civilisation has to eradicate, little by little, with determined perseverance. We are coming to realise the task Atticus has set himself defending Tom.

## Chapter 10

*Summary*

Scout and Jem are embarrassed by Atticus' age which sets him apart from the fathers of their schoolmates; he does not take part in sports and other 'manly' pursuits. They find out, however, when a mad dog runs loose in the neighbourhood, that he is the best shot in Maycomb county. Miss Maudie informs them of this talent which he has kept hidden from them, with her characteristic crisp humour. She then tells them why he never uses this talent, except in emergencies: he feels it gives him an unfair advantage over other living things.

*Commentary*

This chapter presents squarely the idea that people and situations are not always what they seem. This has already been suggested in the presentation of the Cunninghams and of Mr Avery. We find Miss Maudie again at the moral centre of the chapter – as she was in Chapter 5 – and her comment on the action enlightens the children's understanding.

The character of Atticus is further developed for us here. We see him firstly from his children's point of view, as an embarrassment because he is not their idea of what a Southern gentleman ought to be. This opinion is shown to be false when he shoots the mad dog and they hear from Miss Maudie that he is a first class shot. But even before this we have heard Calpurnia's opinion and can see that he is held in respect by the people we have come to trust. While Miss Maudie's comment might sound rather pompous, she is expressing the Christian point of view that talents are a gift from God and should be used to his greater glory and for the benefit of others, rather than for personal advancement. Her comment that Atticus is 'civilised in his heart,' develops one of the major arguments of the novel: what it means to be civilised.

Harper Lee is here presenting Atticus as a truly civilised man, not merely as the product of tradition and convention. Southerners have traditionally considered themselves to be in possession of a unique cultural tradition and to be what is generally regarded as highly civilised. They have ideals of manly courage and courtesy to which Jem refers when he says his father is, after all, a 'gentleman' like himself. Aunt Alexandra, too, takes the traditional point of view when he puts people into categories according to inherited tendencies of social class. The hereditary landowners are seen to be at the top of the social scale and we can understand why the Cunninghams are anxious to hold on to their land at all costs, for to lose it would be to suffer a loss of caste, and even the right to vote. Miss Maudie's statement about Atticus must be seen in this context, for what she means is that Atticus is so much more than what is traditionally understood by the concept civilised. The message here is that being civilised is not only the result of our place in society, our learned attitudes and conventions, but must also involve our hearts as well.

In this chapter the symbolism of the title is emphasised. 'It's a sin to kill a mockingbird', Atticus tells the children and Miss Maudie explains to them what their father means. Mockingbirds are harmless, she tells them, generous creatures who 'sing their hearts out for us'. This gives us our point of reference for the mockingbird symbolism in the novel. Boo Radley and Tom Robinson are both victims of prejudice and thoughtless cruelty: they both sing their hearts out in a sense and are thoughtlessly and cruelly treated. Mockingbirds imitate the songs of other birds and both Boo Radley and Tom Robinson can be seen helping others despite the prejudice against them.

The narrative here is taut with tension and is presented with vivid, visual detail as though Scout were a motion-picture camera. Each picture is set before us and together these make a sequence which culminates in the picture of Atticus as a focal point. When Atticus has accepted the gun from Heck Tate, the sheriff, an almost unbearable suspense is created and the narrative pulls us into the moment and we wait with Scout for the crack of the gun and the release of tension.

## Chapter 11

*Summary*
Jem and Scout go into town to spend Jem's twelfth birthday money. As they pass their neighbour, Mrs Dubose, who is sitting out on her porch, she greets them with her usual viciousness, hurling personal insults at both children and culminating in an attack on Atticus for defending a negro. This provokes Jem to such an extent that on their return from town, he cuts off the heads of every camellia in Mrs Dubose's garden. Atticus sends Jem round to apologise and to tidy up the mess and then he upholds the punishment Mrs Dubose has meted out. Jem is to read to her every afternoon for a month. Jem

protests because her house is dark and creepy; he is afraid to go there. His father has explained why they must try to treat this vicious old lady with courtesy and kindness but it is not until she has died that they learn she was a morphine addict and that Jem's reading provided a distraction while she tried to give up the habit. Atticus presents Mrs Dubose to his children as an example of a truly courageous person, explaining that she wanted to die free of her addiction although this cost her dear in personal suffering.

*Commentary*
This chapter concludes Part I and brings together many of the elements which have been dealt with throughout. It is a suitable time to pause and consider carefully how the themes are being developed as the plot unravels. The previous chapter showed us the different view of their father Scout and Jem were confronted with, and how this changed their opinion of him. This chapter shows them a new side to Mrs Dubose. Both developments in their understanding of people are connected through an awareness of what courage is. This chapter neatly contrasts different kinds of courage: the traditional kind which Atticus displayed and the less obvious kind which he points out in Mrs Dubose. He wants his children to understand that courage is not 'just a man with a gun in his hand' but sometimes requires the determination and perseverance he is trying to point out to them in their neighbour. This courage, which perseveres despite great personal suffering and with no visible reward or acclamation, is the kind he will need himself when he comes to defend Tom Robinson. This episode, placed at the close of Part I, emphasises Atticus' point of view and its importance as a major theme in the novel.

Jem has matured through this experience and has, especially, learned to control his feelings: 'Through the weeks he had cultivated an expression of polite and detached interest which he would present to her in answer to her most blood-curdling inventions.' Scout loyally accompanies her brother and through this experience the children are given the opportunity to 'climb' into Mrs Dubose's 'skin' in order to understand her better. The patience and fortitude they need themselves to face this rather harrowing experience each day, is a small echo of Mrs Dubose's own struggle. As she labours to be free of her addiction, they too are learning a new freedom. Jem especially, is no longer a slave to his feelings but is developing a new maturity which leads him to judge others less harshly.

The emphasis on courage and understanding here enables us to carry the impact this makes into Part II and into the trial, which is the centre of the novel. We will there find these qualities sadly lacking

and come to realise the tragic consequences of this lack. Part I may
be looked upon as a kind of prelude to the trial, where children's
games 'mock' the dangerous adult games the people of Maycomb are
prepared to play with human life. The lessons Scout and Jem have
learned are all preparation for their survival of this event.

## PART II

### Chapter 12

*Summary*
Scout's life is disrupted and she feels miserable. Jem is maturing and
Scout feels cut off from him. Calpurnia shows understanding and
comforts Scout as best she can but Dill is not coming for the summer
and Scout realises how much she misses him. Atticus, too, is
unavailable as he has been called away on business.

Calpurnia decides to take the children to the negro church with her
on Sunday and here they are made very welcome after an uncomfort-
able moment. 'This church has no better friend than your daddy,' the
Reverend Sykes tells them and the children realise for the first time
that Calpurnia has a life apart from them, among her own people
with whom she even speaks a different language. They learn some
more about Tom Robinson as the collection is taken for Helen,
Tom's wife. When they return home they find Aunt Alexandra
waiting for them on the porch.

*Commentary*
In Part 1 we have had the positive values of tolerance and sympathy
presented to us through the lessons the children learn by experience.
Here these values are seen to be an integral part of the negro
community, a warm, cohesive group held together by a leader they
respect. When Lula criticises Calpurnia for bringing white children to
a negro church, Calpurnia responds with 'It's the same God ain't it?'
This simple statement drives home the implications of prejudice.
Those whom Maycomb society treats contemptuously as inferiors
are, in fact, fellow Christians. Irony is used effectively in this chapter
and is highlighted by considerable humour. The negroes emerge as
poor and uneducated people who, nonetheless, make personal
sacrifices to help one another. Through this experience Scout and
Jem learn once again that people are not always what they seem:
Calpurnia is discovered to have a life of her own which is separate
from her life with the Finches. Among her own people she talks their
language instead of the 'educated' English she speaks among the

white people. When Scout asks why, Calpurnia explains that to do otherwise would be 'out of place'. This stresses that there is not right or wrong way to speak but that each community has its own way of speaking, and following from this, its own customs and way of life.

Calpurnia's sense of what is appropriate also demonstrates her natural tact. She is seen here as a much respected, warmly human person and while we can accept this and love her for her fine qualities, the sympathetic portrayal of the whole of the negro community must be seen as unbalanced. The negroes are not presented realistically, but idealistically, although this imbalance is offset to some extent by Atticus' later comment that there is good and bad in all races. In the novel, however, we do not see that this is so. This could leave the author open to an accusation of bias, especially in a novel which warns against prejudices of all kinds, but you may feel that the sympathetic portrayal of the negroes is necessary to counterbalance the contempt in which they are generally held in the novel. It could also be argued that they are no more unrealistically portrayed than Atticus who is presented as a new kind of hero. It is necessary to consider characterisation closely in this respect, and to decide to what extent the general 'niceness' of the negroes and the general 'nastiness' of the whites is simplified in order to contrast with the accepted point of view of the time. What is the effect of this simplification? Some will find it an irritating flaw, others will accept it quite happily.

Whatever we feel about this aspect of the negro community, the chapter prepares us to meet Tom Robinson who is a faithful and respected member of First Purchase Church.

## Chapter 13

*Summary*
With the arrival of Aunt Alexandra, the children are subjected to her opinions and prejudices. They hear from her that every family has inherited tendencies which are apparent as 'Streaks', and the argument about 'Fine Folks' begins here with Aunt Alexandra's suggestion that the longer a family had been squatting on one patch of land the finer it was. More of the history of Maycomb is recounted and the origins of its caste system are explained. Aunt Alexandra fits into Maycomb 'like a hand into a glove' and she causes the children some distress when she wishes, and tries, to mould them according to its prejudices. Atticus is asked by his sister to try and instil in his children some kind of family pride and he makes a bungling attempt to do so but gives up when he sees that his children are becoming

upset. Scout, once again, does not realise until later in life what her father was trying to do, and this reminds us that the story is told in retrospect. This is a well-placed reminder, for the history of Maycomb and its inhabitants would not have been told in this way by a child.

*Commentary*
The previous chapter portrayed the character of Calpurnia in a sympathetic way as an example of the negro community and this chapter, in contrast, portrays Aunt Alexandra satirically as an example of white Maycomb society. Chapter 13 should be read with the previous chapter very much in mind as its full impact depends upon contrasts apparent within both.

The most obvious contrast is between the characters of Calpurnia and Aunt Alexandra. In Chapter 12 we saw Calpurnia as a representative of warm, human values and as a woman who worked to overcome obstacles. She educated her son from the Bible and 'Blackstone's Commentaries', which are an exposition of English law, hardly a suitable book for a beginner! These were the only books available to her and there was no school or any other opportunity for education. This presents her in a very favourable light and we respect her.

Aunt Alexandra's 'river-boat, boarding school manners', are contrasted with Calpurnia's sensitivity to people and to situations. Calpurnia does not give herself airs by speaking educated English among her own people, and does not think it necessary to 'tell all you know', whereas Aunt Alexandra not only 'tells' but expects everyone to agree with her. Here we have a contrast of attitudes; one accepts people as they are and adapts to them, the other criticises all differences and imposes upon people a rigid set of values. It is obvious that the author wishes us to make this comparison and find Aunt Alexandra's attitude wanting.

Calpurnia's warmth towards the children, seen throughout Part I and again in Chapter 12, is also contrasted with Aunt Alexandra's attitude towards them. She has come to look after Scout and Jem out of a sense of duty, rather than a feeling of affection and concern, and the children are not reassured by her presence but are first dismayed and then distressed.

The message here seems to be that those qualities which Calpurnia shows, and which Aunt Alexandra lacks, are necessary if people are to live together in harmony. They are qualities that reassure and bind people together, whereas Aunt Alexandra's rigid standards are divisive. In this chapter the white people of Maycomb are presented in their differences, while in Chapter 12 the negro community was presented as a 'solid mass of coloured people' which perhaps suggests their cohesiveness. There was no caste system here, nor any need to conform to artificial standards of behaviour.

## Chapter 14

### Summary

The children become aware that the Finches are out of favour in Maycomb. Aunt Alexandra and Atticus quarrel over Calpurnia after they hear about the children's visit to First Purchase Church. Jem tells Scout not to antagonise their aunt but she resents his bossiness and fights him. As they go to bed, Scout treads on something and thinks there is a snake under her bed. It turns out be Dill who has run away from home because he thinks his parents are not interested in him and prefer him out of the way. He is allowed to stay and when he later crawls into Scout's bed, they talk about 'getting a baby' as he has heard about a man from whom they can be obtained. The chapter ends with Scout asking Dill why Boo Radley has never tried to run away, to which Dill replies that maybe he has nowhere to run.

### Commentary

The contrasts between Calpurnia and Aunt Alexandra are brought to a head here when Atticus and his sister quarrel about the children's upbringing. Aunt Alexandra insists Calpurnia should leave but Atticus disagrees and tells his sister that he has a very high opinion of her. He also reminds his sister that the children love Calpurnia.

One of the themes of the novel is family life. Atticus' comments about the way his children are being brought up contrast with what we hear of Dill's family background. Dill feels he is an outsider in his parents' home, that they are better off without him, while Jem and Scout have the affection and care not only of their father but also of Calpurnia, whom they love. Scout cannot understand Dill's pathetic speech because what he is trying to tell her seems quite impossible. Another example of unhappy family life is brought to mind when Dill mentions Boo. Dill's understanding of Boo's position to some extent connects the two characters and we feel that Dill is lucky to have the Finches while Boo has nobody at all.

## Chapter 15

### Summary

One evening a crowd of men arrive at the Finches' house to speak to Atticus. They are apprehensive because Tom Robinson is to be lodged overnight in Maycomb jail. Jem is afraid a 'gang' has come for

Atticus but his father reassures him. Later Scout realises Jem is not getting ready for bed as usual and Jem tells her he is going out for a while. Eventually all the children leave together and discover Atticus sitting in front of Maycomb jail reading a newspaper. He has heeded the warning and is protecting Tom. As the children watch, a group of men appear and challenge Atticus, insisting he move and give them access to Tom Robinson, but Atticus refuses. Importunately, Scout bursts into the confrontation, not understanding what it is about and Jem and Dill follow, refusing to leave when asked. Jem is grabbed by one of the men and Scout springs to his defence. She recognises Walter Cunningham's father and begins a friendly conversation which breaks the tension and results in Mr Cunningham sending his lynch mob home. As Atticus thanks his children, Mr Underwood, owner of the *Maycomb Tribune*, reveals himself at the window above his office. He had Atticus covered with his shotgun all the time.

*Commentary*

Like Chapter 10, this chapter is taut with tension and is narrated with the same vivid, visual detail. It is also worth studying for the way the atmosphere is built up and the suspense sustained for the confrontation which forms the dramatic centre of the chapter.

This chapter opens with a description of a homely, family scene at the Finches' house which is interrupted by a group of men apprehending trouble because Tom Robinson has been moved to Maycomb jail for the night before the trial. This is the first dramatic event and tension is built up as Jem, having turned out the light, stands glued to the window watching what is happening outside. Scout and Dill take another window. The tension increases as they strain to catch what the men are saying, and Jem's nervous state is obvious in his impatient waving away of Scout's unspoken question and the way he jumps when the telephone rings. Atticus' cool matter-of-factness dispels the tension both inside and outside the house and the men laugh at Jem's panic.

While the children's action enables them to grasp some idea of what is happening, much of what is said is inaudible as the men kept their voices down. Only an uneasy understanding is achieved and this contributes to the tension and helps, too, to keep the episode realistic, as does Aunt Alexandra's disapproval of the light being out and the eavesdropping.

This dramatic episode prefigures the later one outside the jail, where the children again watch and listen, with every nerve strained, their perception heightened in the darkness. But in the later episode it is Scout, not Jem, who 'jumps' and eventually breaks the tension.

Unlike Jem, who believes the worst in the earlier confrontation, Scout naïvely assumes that Mr Cunningham will respond in a a friendly way to her overtures and she is outraged when Jem is set upon by one of the men. Here the humanitarian themes of the novel are rein-forced and Mr Cunningham's response to Scout, his change of heart, suggests that first 'baby-step' which Miss Maudie refers to. Here one of the first steps in the novel is taken towards overcoming prejudice, and it leads to others, for it is a Cunningham, we discover later, who votes against the Guilty verdict at Tom Robinson's trial. Not only has Mr Cunningham been made to think twice about lynching Tom, he has influenced his relatives. Some readers find this episode unrealistic or even sentimental, but preparation has been made for it earlier in the novel, by the careful description of the Cunninghams' attitudes and way of life.

Atticus' integrity is obvious here, his stand for what he believes in despite great personal danger. His principles and his determination to uphold them are thrown into relief in this chapter, which is ugly with racial prejudice and taut with unspoken threats. While the defence of Tom Robinson has formed a background to the children's adventures so far, and the extent of racial prejudice in Maycomb has been gradually revealed, it is now to become the most important issue. We find that much of what has come before has been leading us towards this point. We are now in a position to understand what a formidable, even impossible, task Atticus has set for himself and why he considers he has been licked a hundred years before he even begins. It is with this in mind that we go forward to the trial.

## Chapter 16

*Summary*
Atticus tells the children at breakfast the next day that Scout was able to influence Mr Cunningham because a mob is always made up of people. However ready to act like wild animals, members of a mob are 'still human'. He suggests that maybe they need a 'police force of children'.

With this in mind we see the county people travelling some distance to Tom's trial, much as the Romans would travel to watch the Christians being thrown to the lions. Miss Maudie is not going to the trial, we hear, and note this as another point in her favour. We meet Dolphus Raymond and learn something of his history and his kind heart. He is a rich landowner but lives with a coloured woman by whom he has half-caste children, 'mixed children' who are sad, Jem tells Scout, because they belong neither to one community nor the other. When the children, instructed by Atticus to stay at home,

arrive at the courthouse it is so full they cannot get in but they are
rescued by Reverend Sykes who finds them seats in the negro gallery.
A description of Judge Taylor concludes the chapter and sets the tone
for the events about to begin.

*Commentary*
Many elements of the novel are pulled together here, reminding us of
the values the author wishes to uphold. Courage is one of these. It
was brought to our attention in the previous chapter and we have now
come to realise the kind of courage Atticus is showing through his
course of action. In Chapter 3 he told Scout, 'You never really
understand a person . . . until you climb into his skin and walk
around in it', and we are reminded of this when he tells them they made
Walter Cunningham stand in his shoes for a minute. It was enough to
avert disaster and Atticus' comment about a police force of children is
one we carry into the courtroom with us, and remember when Dill
cries.

We are reminded how backward the South is with regard to the
negroes when Dolphus Raymond's history is recounted. He is a rich,
white landowner but is isolated from the white community by his
relationship with a coloured woman. The values of the North are
contrasted with those of the South in this chapter as Dolphus sends
his half-caste children North because 'They don't mind 'em up there'.
At this crucial juncture of the novel we are reminded of the negroes'
position in Maycomb society, of their lack of education and opportunity, and that this is not universal. The kindness of Dolphus and
Reverend Sykes reinforces the picture of the negro community
presented in Chapter 12, a community to which the accused belongs.

The comment that Atticus means to defend Tom, not go through a
mockery of a trial in which the verdict is a foregone conclusion, is a
lear example of the attitudes we will meet inside the courtroom. The
children's presence in the coloured gallery puts them, physically,
where Jem and Dill later find themselves in spirit, weeping for the
injustice and inhumanity they witness.

## Chapter 17

*Summary*
The trial begins with the testimony of Heck Tate, the sheriff, who
describes how he was called out by Mr Bob Ewell who told him his
daughter, Mayella, had been raped by a 'nigger'. He recounts how he

found Mayella lying on the floor, beaten up. She told him it was Tom Robinson who hurt her and that he had raped her. Atticus wants to know if a doctor was called and he spends some time questioning Mr Tate about the extent and exact nature of Mayella's injuries, especially wanting to know if it was her right or left eye that had been hurt. Mr Bob Ewell is next in the witness box and he gives evidence in such an offensive way that Judge Taylor has to use his gavel a lot and caution him for his coarseness of expression. Mr Ewell's evidence is much the same as the sheriff's, and Atticus uses the same line of questioning, but this time, having established that it was Mayella's right eye that was hurt, he demonstrates that Bob Ewell is left-handed. Scout sees that this could mean Bob Ewell beat up his daughter himself, Jem is excited and optimistic, but Scout thinks his optimism is premature.

*Commentary*
This is the first of the three trial scenes that occupy this and the following four chapters. The trial is presented in a simple, direct and colloquial style, the dramatic tension controlled through the dialogue. The shifts of mood and atmosphere are accurately observed. Liveliness of expression and acute observation are evident in the sketch of Mr Gilmer and the author's ability to convey the atmosphere of place is evident in the description of the Ewells' cabin and surroundings. This description suggests not only the physical environment of the Ewells, but their emotional and spiritual landscape as well.

We are shown the trial through the careful camera of Scout's observant eye, detailing every tiny movement in a slow-motion technique which has been used before in Chapter 10, and heightens the tension by slowing down the action, keeping us in suspense. We watch each successive action with Scout, detail by detail. Sounds are also presented with vivid immediacy and contribute substantially to the atmosphere, and imagery is used effectively here, to add important emotional colour.

We see how prejudice is at work as soon as Mr Tate gives evidence. When Mayella identified Tom as her attacker, the sheriff did not doubt that this was so, he took her at her word: 'She identified him as the one, so I took him in. That's all there was to it,' he tells Atticus. This matter-of-factness is exploded, however, when Bob Ewell is in the witness box, but the racial implications are the same: a white man or woman's word against a negro's word leaves no room for doubt. The accused is firmly established as only a 'nigger', despite the differences in language used, and the verdict is a foregone conclusion.

The chapter gives us a fine portrait of Bob Ewell, both through Scout's perception of him and through his own words and misunderstandings. We see he is a brutal, inhuman man whose only concern is to assert his superiority over the only section of Maycomb society beneath him in the social hierarchy. Yet a deliberate contrast is made here between the Ewells'environment and that of the negroes he so despises, for the negro cabins are 'neat and snug' as the Christmas journey to the dump demonstrates. And the contrast between Bob Ewell's offensive language and the concern of the Reverend Sykes for the moral welfare of the children in the courtroom, also reinforces the irony of Ewell's position. Ewell is seen to be despising people who are portrayed as greatly his superior as human beings, but his cockiness suggests he is well aware of the insecurity of his position and the need to assert himself as vituperatively as he can. He is aware that the other whites despise him.

## Chapter 18

*Summary*

Mayella Ewell is now called to the witness box to give her version of the alleged crime. She bursts into tears and has to be soothed by the judge. She tells the court that she asked Tom Robinson to chop up an old dresser for her and when she went inside to get a nickel for him, he followed her, attacked her and raped her. Atticus questions her in such a way that the deprivations of her life become evident. She has no friends. Her father drinks heavily and the relief cheque never stretches far enough to meet the needs of the family for whom Mayella has to care as their mother is dead. There is not even enough readily available water for washing and the children are never free from disease. Atticus almost persuades her to admit that her father beats her, for his defence of Tom is to be that it was her father who attacked her, not Tom. But Mayella retracts her half-admission. When Atticus asks her to point out the man who injured her, she indicates Tom Robinson who stands up. It becomes obvious that Tom could not have done so for we now see he has a withered and useless left arm, and Atticus has established that the attacker was left-handed. By the end of the chapter the trial seems to be going well and Atticus agrees that the evidence can be wound up during the afternoon.

*Commentary*

In the previous chapter we were given a picture of Bob Ewell and now we meet his daughter and learn, through Atticus' questioning, more about her way of life. We come to view her as a pathetic figure, a victim of fear and a brutalising life-style. She cannot accept that Atticus is not 'mockin' ' her when he speaks too politely and asks about her friends. We see just what a lonely and outcast figure she is. Her accusation that Atticus is 'mockin' ' her echoes the symbolism of the novel's title, but it is also ironic for it is she and her father who are 'mocking' justice in their perjury, just as we later find out that the trial itself is a mockery, a form only, as Tom Robinson was convicted as soon as Mayella opened her mouth and screamed.

Atticus is sensitive to her position and he is loath to hurt her, and we as readers sympathise to some extent as well, although we cannot condone her ultimate responsibility for the death of Tom Robinson. The fact that she washes her face and tends her geraniums suggests that Mayella is not completely brutalised, that she has retained a sufficient grasp of what is decent and desirable to be aware of the enormity of her crime in falsely accusing Tom. The importance of a stable, loving family background in which sound emotional and moral development can take place has been stressed earlier, and we see again here the moral consequences of its absence. But Mayella cannot be excused, and we will come to see that Boo Radley, that other victim of a cruel father, is a gentle and loving man despite his background. Mayella's testimony is realistically presented in her own words, it is full of inaccuracies and contradictions that speak for themselves. But notice how dramatically the moral centre of this episode is presented. When Atticus asks Mayella to point out the man who raped her, Tom Robinson stands up and his withered arm seems to be proof enough that he could not have caused Mayella's injuries. Atticus has pointed out the truth – Tom's innocence. It is a bitter irony that the truth does not 'stand up' in court, for Tom is eventually convicted despite this proof of his innocence.

## Chapter 19

*Summary*
Tom Robinson is now called by Atticus to the witness box and we have evidence of his honesty at once when he admits to a previous conviction for disorderly conduct. We hear that he and Mayella were not strangers, that he would 'tip his hat' as he went by on his way to work, and that he had already done various jobs for her. We hear that on the day the alleged rape took place, Tom was asked in by Mayella to fetch down a box from the top of a wardrobe and when he turned round, she made advances to him, having sent all the children into town to buy ice-cream with carefully saved money. When asked why he worked so hard for Mayella for nothing, Tom makes the

mistake of admitting he felt sorry for her. He is then bullied by Mr Gilmer which upsets Dill so much he leaves the courtroom. During his evidence, Tom shows great chivalry towards Mayella, and his reluctance to repeat Bob Ewell's offensive remark presents him as a sensitive man. He is a complete contrast to his accuser, being both physically and morally superior. When Link Deas interrupts to give Tom a character reference, this rather idealised picture is complete.

*Commentary*
After the evidence of Bob and Mayella Ewell, and our dramatic first encounter with Tom in the previous chapter, he at last stands before us in person to speak for himself. At once we see the impossibility of his raping Mayella as his useless left hand falls off the Bible. He is seen at once as the victim of his colour for we hear how he had to serve thirty days in jail while the other man involved was able to pay his fine and go free. Tom is coloured and therefore poor. Because he is poor he cannot pay his fine.

Tom's evidence is given simply and directly, the facts speaking for themselves. We find everything he says substantiates the respect in which he is held by the negro community. His evidence also completes our picture of Mayella who emerges as the loneliest person in the world, craving affection in her sexual advances to Tom. Scout realises Mayella's position and draws a parallel between her and Boo Radley. Both are condemned by the attitudes of their fathers, both suffer a life of isolation, unable to take their proper place in the world, both attempt in their own ways to make human contact.

Tom's evidence is realistically idiomatic and should be studied alongside other types of language in the novel. It is his simple idiom that gives his evidence its directness and presents him as an honest and straightforward man. The way Mr Gilmer takes advantage of this is what upsets Dill so much. It is because Mr Gilmer bullies Tom and puts him into a corner that Tom makes the mistake of admitting he felt sorry for Mayella, an answer extremely offensive to the white community. To them it does not suggest kindness or good nature, but an insulting disrespect. How dare a negro feel sorry for a white girl, even if she is as lonely as Mayella, lives among pigs and belongs nowhere, like a 'mixed' child. Tom was probably the only person who had ever been kind to Mayella and yet, Scout tells us, 'when she stood up she looked at him as if he were the dirt beneath her feet'. Just as her father, living on the dump as he does, insists that the close proximity of the negroes is devaluing his property.

At the close of the chapter, an identification is made between Dill
and that other gentle outsider, Dolphus Raymond, who understands
the way Dill is feeling.

## Chapter 20

*Summary*
Dolphus Raymond offers Dill a drink to comfort him and the children
discover it is Coca Cola he drinks, not whisky as is commonly
supposed. Dolphus tells them he pretends to be an alcoholic so that
Maycomb society can say, 'he can't help himself, that's why he lives
the way he does'. He tells them his secret because they are children
and will understand, and he comments that Dill will soon grow out of
his instinctive reaction to 'the simple hell people give other people'.
When the children return to the courtroom, Atticus is summing up.
Mayella has broken the strict code of her society, he says, and it is her
guilt that makes her accuse Tom. He completes his defence with
Thomas Jefferson's statement, 'all men are created equal' and asserts
that at law this must be so. Finally he implores the jury to do their
duty and return a 'not guilty' verdict. It is at this climax that
Calpurnia appears and walks up the aisle towards Atticus, a note in
her hand.

*Commentary*
Dolphus Raymond's suggestion that it is considered to be a lesser evil
for him to be a drunkard than to love a negro woman is a fine
example of the author's skill at structuring events to give them ironic
significance, or to heighten their impact in order to make a moral
point. Coming as it does between Tom's mistake of admitting he felt
sorry for a white woman, and Atticus' summing up of Mayella's
breach of a strong social code, it throws both these into relief. If
Dolphus Raymond, as a wealthy landowner and a member of a
long-established aristocratic family, becomes a social outcast for
loving a negress, Mayella obviously has a strong motive for falsely
accusing Tom to protect herself.

The Dolphus Raymond episode gives the reader a breathing space
as well as a new perspective, and this heightens the dramatic impact
of the novel's climax which follows. Atticus is representing all the
values the author has asserted are essential for a society to be truly
civilised and humane. His defence of Tom Robinson extends beyond
the boundaries of this particular case to a universality that has been
hinted at in Dolphus' comments about man's inhumanity to man.
Atticus points out that there are good negroes and bad negroes, just

as there is good and evil in every race, and suggests to the jury that if they cannot throw aside their prejudices, they are convicting themselves of failing to uphold the principle of justice. As he makes his final speech, Atticus loosens his clothes, a symbolic gesture representing the loosening of conventional restrictions. This kind of symbolic detail was used in the previous chapter: as the truth about Tom and Mayella was revealed, the court lights came on as if to illuminate the truth.

Calpurnia's arrival here realistically brings the narrative back into the world of the children, who realise she must have come to find them.

## Chapter 21

### Summary
Calpurnia has come with a note from Aunt Alexandra to say the children are missing but Mr Underwood reassures Atticus by pointing them out in the coloured gallery. They are marched home by an indignant Calpurnia to have supper but are allowed by Atticus to return for the verdict. When they return, the jury is still out and as Scout waits in suspense in the packed courtroom for the jury to return, she recalls the morning in February when Atticus shot the mad dog. As they left the court, Jem had been exultant, sure they would win, but Atticus, exhausted, had left his opinion unspoken. When the jury finally return they find Tom Robinson guilty. Jem turns white but Atticus calmly takes his leave, pausing as he does so to speak to Tom. As Atticus passes, all the negroes rise in respect.

### Commentary
In this last of the trial scenes, the climax is reached after a long wait for the jury, a period of acute suspense during which the negroes sit as if in church, with 'biblical patience'. We experience this long wait through Scout's sensations. After experiencing the trial in a more objective way, through the actual interchanges between Atticus and the witnesses, Calpurnia's arrival returns us firmly to the world of the children. This is an anticlimax where the trial is concerned, the pause before the final peak, but a climax for the children who ought to be at home and who realise Calpurnia has come to find them.

Scout's wonderfully evocative description of the waiting courtroom is a fine piece of narrative, and the unnatural stillness of the packed place reminds Scout of the day Atticus shot the mad dog, when the street itself was deserted but the atmosphere was similarly alive with tension. As the jury return, Scout experiences the same distant feeling she felt on that earlier occasion.

Before the verdict was given, Scout knew intuitively what it would
be and she instinctively shuts her eyes as the polling paper is handed
to the judge. But she opens them to 'peek' at Jem, noting his reaction
for us. Jem's white knuckles and the jerk of his shoulders as if he is
being stabbed, establish an empathy between him and Tom Robinson. But Tom, no doubt, expected this verdict as did Atticus, unlike
Jem who is now to suffer a strong reaction in his disillusionment. He
has placed such faith in justice and the law, and only now realises the
trial has been a mockery of justice, and his father's valiant efforts
have been in vain.

It would be a good idea to pause now and consider the effect the
trial has had upon you, as a reader. Try to identify your response as
the trial progressed. Did you, for example, feel like Jem that Atticus
had 'got him' (Chapter 17) when Bob Ewell admitted to being
ambidextrous? How did you feel when Atticus almost made Mayella
admit that her father beat her? (Chapter 18). Did you hope, like Jem,
that justice would prevail after all, or were there enough clues to
suggest that it would not? If you analyse your response in this way, you
will come to a better understanding of the narrative techniques used
throughout the trial scene. Read again, at this point, the episode of
the mad dog (Chapter 10) so that the contrast between the deserted,
February street and the crowded, summer-hot courtroom can be
appreciated, and Scout's reaction to the suspense during both of
these crises can be compared.

## Chapter 22

*Summary*
It is now Jem's turn to cry and his response to the verdict is very
moving. He cannot understand it. Even Aunt Alexandra is affected,
and shows her sympathy by calling Atticus 'brother', something we
have not heard her do before. But although Atticus is too exhausted to
offer Jem any further sympathy, by morning he has regained his usual
balance and is considering the appeal.

The negroes have shown their appreciation of Atticus' stand on
their behalf and have sent piles of food, which suggests the epic quality
of their gratitude just as Scout's description of them in the courtroom
suggested the epic quality of their patience. Dill's response is that he
will be a clown when he grows up as there is nothing to do but laugh at
folk. Miss Maudie has baked them all cakes and suggests that although
Atticus did not win, a 'baby-step' has been taken towards the future for
the jury took a long time to decide what, at one time, they would have
decided in a moment. She tells the children that Judge Taylor had his
reasons for appointing Atticus to defend Tom.

The chapter ends with Miss Stephanie Crawford and Miss Rachel warning the children that danger is coming because Mr Bob Ewell has spat in Atticus' face and sworn to get his revenge.

*Commentary*

This chapter portrays Jem's and Dill's reactions to the verdict which are quite different, but understandable from what we know of their characters. Jem's tears are for the injustice of what he has just experienced. Dill earlier left the courtroom in tears because of Mr Gilmer's inhumanity which Dolphus Raymond universalised with his comment. This contrast stresses Jem's more rational approach – he is the son of a lawyer and desperately wanted to see justice done. Dill's reaction is quite different, however, for the unreasonableness of the situation makes him decide to be a clown and join a circus. Unlike Jem, he no longer expects justice to be done, he views human affairs as absurd and unpredictable. This is the response of an imaginative, sensitive child who prefers to escape from what is painful, unable to bear the harsh reality of what he sees in the adult world.

Miss Maudie's sympathy, shown by the cakes, represents the point of view that life must go on as usual, no matter what. This is tied up with her conviction that things will change slowly but inevitably. She did not expect Atticus to win, she tells the children, but views the long time the jury needed to come to a decision as a 'baby-step' in the right direction. It is interesting to note that she no longer sees Jem as one of the children, baking him his own little cake as she does Scout and Dill. She acknowledges his new maturity by giving him a slice from the adults' cake, and this symbolises Jem's painful emergence into the adult world which has been brought about through his disillusionment.

The close of the chapter, with Miss Stephanie Crawford's news about Bob Ewell, brings a new point of departure and returns the dramatic focus to Jem, Scout and Dill. But the trial is not over for the Finches as Ewell's humiliation in the witness box is to have a sequel, which will lead us to the final climax of the novel.

## Chapter 23

*Summary*

Atticus does not appear to be too concerned about Bob Ewell's threats but the children are afraid for him until he reassures them. Jem has doubts about rape as a capital crime but Atticus tells him it is the death sentence on circumstantial evidence that concerns him. A discussion of the jury system follows. We hear that it was one of the Cunninghams who prevented a quick decision from being made by the jury and Jem appreciates the irony of this. Scout decides to ask

Walter Cunningham to dinner but Aunt Alexandra's ideas about caste do not allow this. When her Aunt refers to Walter as 'trash' Scout is very upset and Jem has to comfort her. A discussion about different types of people follows and Jem asserts that what matters is not 'background' as Aunt Alexandra understands it, the 'Old Family' obsession, but how long a family has been literate. Scout disagrees claiming that everyone is alike. Jem points out that if this were so they would all get on, and he begins to realise why Boo Radley stays inside his house.

*Commentary*
We are reminded here of Atticus' refusal to carry a gun, and that he did not have one even when sitting out his vigil to protect Tom from the lynch mob. His particular brand of courage is stressed here to throw into relief the fear that prevents people from doing what they know is right. Juries are afraid, Atticus tells Jem, and we see that their fear arises from self-interest just as this chapter demonstrates that Atticus' courage stems from the opposite, from tolerance and humanity, virtues characterised by a move towards the interests of others.

Atticus helps the children to stand in Bob Ewell's shoes a moment, and we see that the values posited early in the novel are still being strongly presented in the post-trial period, even though Atticus' courage appears to have been in vain. While he has failed in his attempt to bring in a not-guilty verdict, his values are still clearly untouched by this and he has not given way to bitterness or disappointment as he could so easily have done. Atticus even hopes that Ewell's attack on him might have saved Mayella from a beating. You could ask yourself at this point in the novel, how far you feel his character has been idealised and how much you admire him as a man of principle. Is his one main flaw his over-confidence in human nature, his wrong judgement of Bob Ewell, which nearly has tragic consequences? Should his charitable view of people be a little more cautious and realistic, perhaps?

While Atticus is 'dry' in his response to Ewell, and rational in his discussion with Jem, the strength of his feelings is obvious in his use of the word 'trash' when describing a white man who takes advantage of a negro, a term Aunt Alexandra devalues when using it to speak of Walter Cunningham. Atticus speaks from his heart, Aunt Alexandra from prejudice.

Jem is beginning to understand the inadequacy of the law in dealing with prejudice, which is a hard lesson for him. He was so optimistic when the evidence all pointed to the impossibility of Tom

33

having committed the crime. He is learning that what is so obvious to some, is not so obvious to others, and without the humanity and tolerance that Atticus is showing, facts in themselves are not enough. It is, of course, ironic that a Cunningham should have voted against the verdict when Mr Cunningham was one of the lynch mob, and with enough authority to break it up, but this demonstrates to us how far-reaching Scout's action was on that night. It is also obvious that a connection is to be made between Jem's explosive surprise and Scout's idea of inviting Walter Cunningham home to dinner, forgetting her private resolve to beat him up the next time she saw him. Both changes of heart are intended to be connected.

Aspects of both Jem's immaturity and his development are obvious in this chapter, and the latter can be seen especially in his insights into people and relationships. Boo Radley stays indoors, he realises, because he does not want to come out into a world Jem himself is beginning to find hostile and incomprehensible. His new understanding is also seen in the way he advises Scout not to let her aunt 'aggravate' her. It seemed only yesterday, Scout notes, that he was telling her not to 'aggravate' her aunt.

## Chapter 24

*Summary*
This chapter describes the meeting of the Missionary Society at the Finches' house where Scout is dressed in her Sunday best and helps Calpurnia to serve the ladies. These ladies discuss the 'Mrunas', a jungle tribe, and are dismayed at the hardship of their lives and the way custom still holds its barbaric sway. In the same breath they are discussing American negroes, criticising the Northern States for their liberal attitudes and accusing them of hypocrisy. Atticus arrives unexpectedly and in haste to enlist Calpurnia's help. He must go and tell Helen Robinson that Tom has been shot dead trying to escape from prison.

*Commentary*
This chapter is a fine satire on the ladies of that 'Christian' town in which Mrs Merriweather tells Scout to be grateful she is living. Once again contrasts highlight the moral points the author wishes to make and we appreciate the structuring of events which present the contrasts as effectively as possible. In the previous chapter, Atticus demonstrated the tolerance we have come to accept as the primary message of the novel, while in this chapter we meet hypocrisy, conformity and a further 'mockery' of Christian values.

The description of the Mrunas is also a fair description of Maycomb as we have come to know it. The ladies are moved to tears by the conditions of the poor people J. Grimes Everett is trying to save, people who live in poverty, darkness and immorality, a state which exists right under their dainty, powdered noses, but to which they seem to be oblivious, a state perpetuated by their own tribal customs. All the criticisms they make about the Mrunas have their counterparts in Maycomb society, seen in the stereotyping of Southern women, the breakdown of family life – in the Radleys, in the Ewells and in Dill's relationship with his parents – in Jem's ordeal throughout the trial and in the squalid conditions that some of Maycomb society have to suffer and the disease consequent upon them. Even Judge Taylor's cigar has its counterpart! The chapter is mined with ironies that handsomely repay the trouble it takes to discover them.

Humour, however, lightens the satire and takes the bite out of it. The imagery used to describe Mrs Merriweather's voice and the seemingly innocent remarks Scout makes are good examples. To the ladies, the comments are amusing, but to us they have a wry side. There is humour too, in the description of the ladies' conformity. They are like a herd of well-trained cattle. These ladies are condemned out of their own mouths but Scout's portrayal of them turns the meeting into a pantomime until the arrival of Atticus shows up their behaviour for what it really is. It is because of this kind of hypocritical complacency that Tom is dead. After the ladies' comments that negroes are either immoral or ineducable, Atticus' respect for Calpurnia is here deeply ironic. She is the only person Atticus can turn to for help in his difficult and delicate task.

## Chapter 25

*Summary*
Jem orders Scout to put the roly-poly she has found outside where it belongs instead of crushing it as she intended. Scout views this as yet another sign that Jem is changing and she observes that it is he who is becoming more like a girl, not herself. Dill has returned to Meridian now the summer holidays are over and Scout recalls his description of Helen's reaction to her husband's death. Mr Underwood refers to it as 'senseless slaughter' in the *Maycomb Tribune*. At the close of the chapter we hear that Bob Ewell has not forgotten his threat.

*Commentary*
The neat connection made between Jem's attitude to the roly-poly and the way Dill describes Helen's reaction to Tom's death, is an

example of the careful structuring of small events to transfer moral points into a wider context. Helen was like an insect that had been trodden on, Dill has told Scout, and this very finely suggests not only her own anguish but the position of the negroes in society, deprived of the education and opportunities we generally consider to be 'humanising', crushed to death in a mindless way. This chapter continues to show us Jem's moral development and we find, in the change of heart of Mr Underwood, that Miss Maudie was right when she insisted that more people than the children supposed were anxious to progress towards a more humane society. Mr Underwood hated and despised negroes, he wouldn't have one near him (Chapter 16), but he was prepared to defend Atticus from his office window as Atticus sat protecting Tom from the lynch mob, and now he uses his newspaper to voice his opinion about Tom's death. He writes not about injustice, but about the 'senseless slaughter of songbirds by hunters and children', and in such a way that even children can understand him, although, ironically, his passion is misunderstood by Maycomb people who assume he is trying to be poetical and get himself reprinted in the *Montgomery Advertiser*.

The mockingbird symbolism is obvious here but the chapter also focuses humanitarian principles in both the children's and the adult world. Scout has arrived where many of the people of Maycomb, and her brother, have been for some time and this chapter presents a major development in her understanding.

## Chapter 26

*Summary*
Scout returns to school and the walk past the Radley house reminds her of the adventures they had in connection with Boo, and that Atticus knew far more of these than they realised. She also reviews the changes in their lives and we hear she does not think too much about them, or about people and their peculiarities, unless she is forced to do so. One of these occasions occurs in a Current Events lesson at school, when Hitler is discussed by Miss Gates, the teacher, and Scout is once again mystified by what seem to be the vagaries of human behaviour. She asks Jem his opinion only to find he reacts violently and orders her to be quiet. Atticus comforts Scout and tells her that Jem is going through a difficult time in his life.

*Commentary*
The major thrust of this chapter is Miss Gates' hypocrisy, her criticism of prejudice and her ironic insistence that America is a democracy, which she writes on the blackboard. We are directed towards an

association of Jews and negroes in the humorous mistake of Cecil Jacobs who uses, inadvertently, the wrong word to describe Hitler's actions. We have already seen that in the case of negroes the two words are virtually interchangeable in Alabama. The connections are continued in Miss Gates' description of the Jews as a race who have always been persecuted, and their religious attitudes. We find the negroes similar in both respects. The comment that Jews are white, speaks for itself and reminds us of Scout's fight with Cecil in Chapter 9.

We see in what way Scout and Jem are growing up. Scout has remained relatively unaffected by the trial and its repercussions, not thinking of people and their behaviour very much. Jem, being more mature, has been deeply disturbed and is trying to assimilate his experiences. He is furious with Scout because she is able to voice, in her naïvety, what he has not yet been able to come to terms with.

## Chapter 27

### Summary
Bob Ewell gets a government job but is soon dismissed for laziness. He still bears a grudge as he tries to break into Judge Taylor's house one night and frightens Helen Robinson until Link Deas, her employer, warns him off with a threat of jail. We hear an amusing account of a Hallowe'en prank by Maycomb children and to prevent this happening again, a pageant is being arranged this Hallowe'en at the high-school. Scout is to play the role of Pork.

### Commentary
We are kept in touch with the activities of Bob Ewell and reminded that he has not forgotten his threats, but the tension is lightened with the amusing tale of the Misses Tutti and Frutti and Mrs Merriweather's ideas for the pageant. The chapter functions as a lull before a new storm breaks, but Bob Ewell's behaviour – to the Judge and to Helen – and Aunt Alexandra's unfinished sentence, are both ominous suggestions of what is to come.

## Chapter 28

### Summary
Jem takes Scout to the pageant and they remind themselves of the early days of 'haints' and 'hot steams' which now seem far away in their childhood. Cecil Jacobs jumps out on them as they cross the yard in the darkness and Scout goes off with him while Jem joins the audience. Scout misses her cue in the pageant as she falls asleep and,

embarrassed, she asks Jem to wait until the crowd has dispersed before they leave. On the way home they discover they are being followed and when they have almost reached the safety of the road and the street lamps, they are attacked. An unknown man comes to their rescue and carries the unconscious Jem into the house with Scout following. The doctor and sheriff are called and Scout is reassured that Jem is not dead but has a badly broken arm. Mr Heck Tate tells them that Bob Ewell is lying under a tree, killed by a kitchen knife.

*Commentary*

This chapter is a superb example of the author's narrative skill and should be studied in some detail to identify the elements with which the drama is built. By now the author's technique has become familiar. Carefully observed detail, conveying the sensory perceptions of observant and sensitive children, builds up an atmosphere of suspense. This atmosphere carries symbolic significance and irony is a major component. Finally, there is development towards a moral point.

Here we learn at once that the night is warm and dark. 'There is no moon' is an almost traditional trigger and we expect 'something to happen'. Students of *Macbeth*, for example, will remember that when King Duncan was murdered it was a very dark night and they will recognise the symbolic connection between darkness and evil. There are many examples in literature. Here the darkness is emphasised again and again.

The night is dark and hot, and suggests the tense atmosphere before a thunderstorm which develops the dramatic tension soon to climax under the tree. The illuminated school in the distance, obviously suggests security. Uneasiness is suggested as the children turn and find the lights have gone out behind them, leaving them vulnerable in the darkness. While it provides a cover for Bob Ewell's evil action, and also symbolises the blackness in his heart, this same darkness provides a cover for the children's rescuer, Boo Radley. We have had a prefiguration of Boo's action in the lyrical description of the mockingbird earlier in the chapter, and Cecil Jacobs' appearance with the flashlight and his successful attempt to frighten the children, prefigure just as finely Bob Ewell's attack on them.

## Chapter 29

*Summary*

Aunt Alexandra feels she is to some extent to blame for what has happened as she failed to pay attention to an uneasy feeling she experienced earlier in the evening. The 'pin-prick of apprehension' she now feels should have warned her not to let Jem and Scout go to the pageant alone. Scout gives an account of the evening's events to Mr Tate who realises Scout's costume probably saved her life. He shows them the knife marks on it, and contradicts Atticus who says Ewell was 'out of his mind.' He does not share Atticus' tolerant view of human nature. Scout completes her account with a reference to the man who rescued them. Mr Tate asks who this person was and Scout points to the unknown man in the corner of the room who carried Jem home. The chapter concludes with a description of this man who Scout realises is Boo Radley.

*Commentary*
The most important event of this chapter is Scout's intuitive recognition of Boo Radley to whom her account of the night's events inevitably turns. Here is the climax of all the children's attempts to make Boo 'come out'. He has done so in order to save their lives. Compare the physical description of Boo here with Jem's fanciful description in Chapter 1 where he is likened to a fearsome wild animal. Nothing could be further from the truth and the two descriptions make as stark a contrast as it is possible to make. In the one Boo is fierce and savage, in the other he is frail, timid and gentle. It is Bob Ewell who is like the wild animal, emboldened by drink to attack children.

Scout's recognition of Boo comes when she has given up all hope of ever seeing him. In Chapter 26 she recollected their early connections – the presents in the oak tree and all their attempts to make contact. She is old enough now to realise that the last thing he wants is to be spied on. She had been content with things the way they were but for the last time fantasised briefly once more about passing his house one day and seeing him on the porch. But she knew it was only a fantasy and was reconciled to the fact that they would never meet. Now they do meet for the first time and Scout weeps.

Boo's colour is deliberately emphasised here: 'they were white hands, sickly white hands' and 'His face was as white as his hands.' His whiteness is here emphasised in the same way that Tom's blackness was emphasised in the courtroom: 'Tom was a black-velvet Negro, not shiny, but soft black velvet. The whites of his eyes shone in his face, and when he spoke we saw flashes of his teeth.' Boo and Tom are shown almost as the negative and the positive of the same image. *Black* and *white* are thus associated, an important connection because Boo and Tom are also connected through the mockingbird imagery:

both are victims of cruel and senseless prejudice. Scout picks up the connection between Boo and Tom in the next chapter, but this is, for the reader, the climax of association between the two. Here is the moral point towards which the last two chapters have been leading.

## Chapter 30

*Summary*
Scout is gently reminded of her manners but is astounded at the casual way both Atticus and Dr Reynolds speak to Boo, as if it was the most natural thing in the world. But she soon finds herself acting in a similar way. As Atticus has shown consideration for Boo in Jem's room by not bringing him a chair, and does so again in suggesting they all remove to the porch when Dr Reynolds asks them to leave while he examines Jem, so Scout too finds herself behaving in the same way, and she finds him a dark corner. Atticus thinks Heck Tate wants to cover up Jem's crime – he assumes it was Jem who killed Bob Ewell – and there is a battle of wills between the two men until Atticus finally grasps the truth. It is Boo, not Jem, whom Mr Tate wishes to protect by insisting Bob Ewell fell on his knife. Scout understands at once what the sheriff is trying to do.

*Commentary*
Atticus' principles are the main element of this chapter as he insists that he can't live one way in town and another way in his home. His feelings about his relationship with his children are made clear here. Previously we have seen his children's feelings about their relationship with him. Compare Atticus' insistence that is is essential that Jem respects him with Jem's rather inarticulate explanation to Scout in Chapter 6. It is obvious that both Atticus and Jem respect one another and want to live up to what is expected of them. Atticus substantiates Scout's declaration to Dill in Chapter 14 too, where she told Dill that Atticus could not do without her, that he needed her. It is perhaps ironic that Atticus' optimistic view of human nature – one of his finest qualities – almost costs him what he holds most dear. He is also concerned that Jem shall not escape justice because he is a lawyer's son and fails to understand what Scout here grasps at once.

Because Boo killed Bob Ewell in self-defence, or to protect the children's lives, Heck Tate realises how cruel it would be to drag him into a public court. When he insists that Ewell's death was an accident, he is enacting what Atticus professed in Chapter 3. This is fine irony because it was on the Ewells' behalf that Atticus was prepared to bend the law earlier.

# Chapter 31

*Summary*

Scout leads Boo into Jem's room so that he can 'say' goodnight to him, and she encourages him to pet Jem when he seems wary of doing so. Boo asks Scout if she will take him home and she does so, making him take her arm so that it would seem to any onlooker that he was escorting her, not the other way round. Scout stands on the Radley porch and surveys the street from Boo's vantage point, seeing what he must have seen over the past two years, looking out from behind his shutters. When she returns home she finds Atticus reading Jem's book *The Grey Ghost* and she asks him to read to her, which he does. Scout falls asleep but insists, as Atticus puts her to bed, that she heard the whole story. It was about a boy who turned out to be 'real nice' when everybody had got to know him. Most people are, Atticus tells the sleepy Scout, 'when you finally get to know them'.

*Commentary*

Scout's sensitivity towards Boo is evident when she realises he wants to pet Jem, and again when she gallantly offers him her arm on the way back to the Radley place so that he will not be shamed by his need to be escorted. Scout's actions substantiate Dolphus Raymond's faith in children and their ability to understand his secret. Children sometimes have an intuitive understanding, the author seems to be suggesting here, and Scout and Dill have certainly demonstrated this tendency on occasions throughout the novel.

Atticus is prepared to sit up all night in Jem's room so that when his son wakes he will be there to comfort and reassure him. This is the final example of the warmth and security enjoyed, and taken for granted, by Scout and Jem in their family life. It is interesting to note that Atticus uses the time to get to know his children better, by reading the books that they read, finding in them the message he has being trying to convey.

So the novel begins and ends with Jem. This emphasises his place in the narrator's world, he is the 'born hero' around whom Scout's life has revolved during her childhood. It also points to Jem as the 'hero' of the novel because in his development from a child into an adult, we find hope for future Maycombs. Even as Scout is entering a new phase of growth and maturity, we find that Jem has already travelled further on his journey, leaving behind the boyhood to which Boo Radley touchingly pays tribute for the first and last time. Perhaps an identification between Jem and Tom is intended in the injured left arm, just as an identification was made between them in the courtroom as Jem flinched under the stab of words which killed Tom.

n's chances' (Chapter 24) and tries to make a break.
om Nathan Radley who mistakes him for a negro
m left only his trousers on the fence. Tom in his escape,
It is the dehumanising process of categorising people that
is anxious to criticise here. Even when Tom has paid with
s attitude is evident. 'Tom's death was typical. Typical of a
cut and run.'
rough the voice of Miss Maudie, through her tribute to
d her optimism, that we hear the voice of the truly civilised,
Christian. There may not be many people in Maycomb who
erned about the lot of the negroes but there are some who
not only the whites should be treated fairly. Miss Maudie lays
ress on 'the handful' of people who do not follow current
g and is optimistic in the face of defeat. She sees the length of
at Atticus was able to keep the jury out as a positive move
d and she also points out that it was no accident that Judge
r chose Atticus to defend the case. Not all of Maycomb society
the negroes like outcasts, and it is the behaviour and attitudes
ese people who provide the contrast and enable us to see what
and should, be done to remove this particular 'hell'.
the novel we also find the *hell of family life*. Three examples of
ily life can be seen to contrast with the warm security of the
ches. Arthur Radley is the victim of a bigoted and proud father
o sacrifices his son's emotional and physical health to his own
ejudices. Shut away from all human contact in a veritable 'hell' of
neliness to which he eventually adapts, turning it into a shell to
rotect his impaired personality, Arthur does attempt to make some
kind of human contact – with the Finch children. His brother Nathan
turns out to be as cruel as his father, however, and by filling up the
hole in the tree with cement, effectively prevents the developing
relationship from continuing. This family with its 'secrets' and its
closed shutters, demonstrates the damage that can be done when
human beings are deprived of the emotional environment they need
to grow to their full potential.

Mayella Ewell is another example. Her life, too, is made hell by a
father who cares nothing for her development, physical, emotional or
moral, forcing her into a brutal way of life. While we cannot condone
her lies, we can sympathise with her as an impaired human being and
compare her lack of opportunity, her lack of a moral education,
with the upbringing Scout and Jem are receiving. Unlike Dolphus
Raymond, who is a rich landowner, Mayella breaks the social code
not by choice, but out of desperation. She has no friends. She is
starved of affection and this is the only way she knows how to seek it.
She overcomes her prejudices against the negroes only long enough

The use of the word 'stab' in this context prefigures the final climax of
the novel, and Jem, in a sense, inherits Tom's injured arm as
his legacy.

Atticus' final comment to Scout that when you finally 'see' or
understand people, most of them turn out to be 'real nice' just like
the boy in the story – despite the fact that so many of the whites in
the novel appear to be anything but 'real nice' – is the author's final
thrust. Despite Ewell's behaviour and Atticus' misjudgement of his
nature, we are directed towards an optimistic view of human nature
and a stance that is prepared to find the best in people and build upon
it towards a better future. Jem and Scout have come to 'see' people as
they really are and are able to understand better what causes pain and
injustice in the world. This is finely compressed in Scout's observa-
tions from the Radley porch. You must decide for yourself whether
you find Atticus' comment to Scout naïve and unrealistic, or whether
you find it an example of his generous heart and optimistic view of
human nature, justified by the community's 'baby step' forward
which the events of Maycomb over these past two years have
accomplished.

# 3 THEMES AND ISSUES

## 3.1 INTRODUCTION

*To Kill a Mockingbird* is concerned with many themes unified into the moral landscape of a small town. Within the novel we live for a while in Maycomb and get to know its inhabitants, some of them intimately. We begin to understand the moral tone of the town with its hypocrisies, its self-interest, its fear of change. Most importantly, we come to understand its prejudices. Many ideas – about courage, racial prejudice, religious bigotry, family life, democracy, education, childhood – can be combed out to be looked at separately. But all these ideas work together to present the author's firm conviction that only through a slow evolution, through the education of the feelings and sensibilities of the next generation, can real development towards a better society take place.

The author portrays in Atticus what she considers to be a truly civilised man, but at the same time, satirises those qualities and values that pass as civilised, 'mocking' or imitating the real thing. It is through this contrast between what is good and what is not, that the themes of the novel are made evident. Each event or episode is carefully placed in a sequence of events so that its implications are given the greatest possible impact. We find ourselves constantly making comparisons as we read, and it is thus we realise the moral messages of the novel. Atticus is portrayed as a true Christian and a true gentleman, but not according to the ideas prevalent at the time. It is by contrasting his behaviour with the behaviour of other members of Maycomb society that we come to understand what the author means by 'civilised', 'Christian' and 'gentleman'. One of the purposes of the novel is to redefine these concepts.

While it is the moral world of Maycomb we are concerned with in the novel, the issues here are not confined only to this particular time

and place. We can transfer the [...] world we live in and find they a[...] its universality and perhaps acco[...] read by successive generations thr[...]

## 3.2 MAN'S INHUMANITY TO MA[...]

One of the most obvious contrasts in [...] Maycomb's inhabitants have every char[...] have no chance at all. Dolphus Raymo[...] Robert Burns (the eighteenth-century Sco[...] inhumanity to man', in a poem with the t[...] made to mourn'. This certainly seems to [...] Maycomb's inhabitants, especially the negro[...]

There are many examples of this 'hell' [...] outcast, of being denied what is necessary [...] human growth and happiness, but probably the /[...] is the dominant theme. The negroes have no edu[...] ties. We learn that Calpurnia has taught her son 2[...] the bible and a law book, *Blackstone's Commentari[...] only available resources. The use of this book is i[...] the way law is 'mocked' in the trial of Tom Robins[...] reminder of the illiteracy of the blacks is evident in the [...] which fascinates Scout, who was 'born reading the M[...] (Chapter 2). Zeebo's job also gives us some idea of the [...] job prospects for blacks as he is a dustman and consider[...] good job for a negro. We find out that the blacks' [...] depressed. Mrs Merriweather pays her girl Sophy a tiny [...] expects her to be cheerful all the time, even after Tom's co[...] By 'cheerful' Mrs Merriweather seems to imply 'grateful'. [...] example of the way they are treated as employees is evident [...] way the Missionary Society ladies enjoy Calpurnia's cooking bu[...] her as if she doesn't exist (Chapter 24).

We constantly hear the blacks derided and insulted. At best [...] are referred to as 'niggers' and considered to be ineducable, at w[...] they are all viewed as immoral and potentially criminal. When accus[...] of a crime they are not even considered worthy of a fair trial, as th[...] lynch mob and Cecil Jacobs' relayed remark make all too painfully [...] clear (Chapter 9).

The image Dill uses to describe Helen's reaction when told of [...] Tom's death, sums up the way the whites treat the blacks. This [...] suggests not only the brutal way they are treated but how invisible [...] they are as people. Nathan Radley can shoot at them with impunity [...] (Chapter 6), and this forecasts the shooting of Tom when he is 'tired

of white ma[...] Escaping fr[...] intruder, Je[...] left his life.[...] Harper Lee[...] his life, thi[...] nigger to [...] It is th[...] Atticus a[...] the truly [...] are cond[...] say that [...] great s[...] thinkin[...] time t[...] forwa[...] Taylo[...] treat[...] of th[...] can [...]

to trap Tom Robinson in the machine which grinds him inexorably to his death. But perhaps she might have been prevailed upon to tell the truth if she had not lived in such mortal fear of her father. Scout compares Mayella to a 'mixed' child who belongs nowhere (Chapter 19). Arthur Radley remained essentially a child in his isolation, drawn towards children. Mayella craves a man's love and has no chance of winning it. There are suggestions in the novel that her father has forced her into an incestuous relationship with him, a further degradation to which she submits out of fear.

Dill too is lonely. He tells Scout that his people get on better without him but he is the lucky one of the three family casualties. He is able to adopt the Finches. This is made very clear when he has run away from home and is found hiding under Scout's bed (Chapter 14). He is given material things by his mother and stepfather but, like Mayella and Arthur Radley, is starved of love. Arthur is deprived of parental love and eventually of all contact with other people; Mayella is a 'mock' wife for her father, living in a no-man's land; Dill is an invisible son, shut out from his parents' real life.

In her treatment of family life, Harper Lee demonstrates not only the hell of loneliness suffered by these unfortunates in contrast to the warm relationships enjoyed by Scout and Jem, but also the tragic results of their situation. Her message here is that mutual love and respect are necessary for the emotional, physical and moral development of children into sound, well-balanced adults, into people who will in their turn be able to ameliorate in some small way, the injustices of their particular world.

There is also the *hell of class consciousness* which keeps sections of the community in isolation from one another. This is evident throughout the novel and can be seen to permeate the entire fabric of Maycomb society. Only those characters whom we consider to be the most enlightened seem to be free of it. We also find that it is dealt with ironically, adding depth to the position of the blacks. Calpurnia, herself a deprived member of Maycomb society on account of her colour, is able to reprimand Scout about her treatment of Walter Cunningham at lunch, commenting that social position is of no consequence if the responsibilities that go with it are ignored. Scout is ingrained with the town's hierarchical attitudes, and she tells Calpurnia that Walter is not 'company', that he cannot be considered a guest, because he is only a Cunningham. Later on, however, we find she has been educated out of this point of view and is deeply upset when Aunt Alexandra refers to Walter as 'trash'.

Many examples of the 'hell' of class consciousness are evident in the novel and we see how this contributes to the damage already inflicted on the community by racial prejudice. Maycomb is a strictly structured society and we see through the attitudes of Aunt Alexandra, the real state of affairs in social relationships. Until she arrives, the Finch family are not concerned with this aspect of Maycomb life, but their aunt, with her 'river-boat, boarding school manners', tries to impress on the children the family pride she herself feels. They are 'the product of several generations' gentle breeding,' she tells them, and they should live accordingly, mixing only with people of equal social status. She is shocked by the way they are being brought up, finding poor whites such as the Cunninghams not fit company for them. She is horrified to hear that Calpurnia took them to church with her where they mixed with the black community, and that Scout has asked to visit Calpurnia's home.

Aunt Alexandra is amusing when she categorises people and describes each family's 'Streak', but she holds the traditional point of view that it is the hereditary landowners who have the highest social status, a point of view Scout tries to undermine by referring to the Ewells. Jem decides that it is education that matters. When Atticus confronts his children at his sister's insistence, and tries to explain about family pride, he causes them so much upset and alarm that he abandons his attempt. Like Miss Maudie, he believes that it is a person's moral worth that is important, not his social status and this one of the important messages of the novel. Harper Lee's plea here is for people to lay aside the divisive trappings of class and status, to be like Atticus, described by Miss Maudie as 'civilised in his heart' (Chapter 10).

## 3.3  EXTENDING OUR SYMPATHIES

An antidote to the hell that people give other people is the formula offered to Scout by her father in Chapter 3. It is a simple trick, he tells her, which will enable her to get on better with 'all kinds of folks'. Throughout the novel we feel the author's conviction that through this 'trick', sympathies will be extended and society will become a better place. Characters in the novel are judged by how well they can make this imaginative leap.

Scout has her first lesson in tolerance when Atticus teaches her what a compromise is. He suggests to her that it is better on occasions to bend the law to serve people than to hurt people through its assiduous application. The example he gives is that the Ewell children would go hungry if their father was prosecuted for hunting out of season. The message here is that rules and regulations are, like codes and conventions, to help, not to stunt, the process of civilisation. Scout must learn what lies behind a person's behaviour, must come to understand the reasons why he acts the way he does before jumping to conclusions and making judgements. Many examples reinforce this point: Miss Caroline misunderstands Scout because she is a stranger to Maycomb's ways, Mrs Dubose is venomously spiteful because she is sick, Mayella tells lies because she is afraid.

This is an essential lesson for Scout, part of the fine moral education she is receiving from her father. It is also one of the cornerstones of the novel. The message here is that if tolerance and understanding can be developed at this level, prejudices will be overcome and justice and equality will be slowly achieved in society. The children have many opportunities to use this 'simple trick', opportunities which prepare them for disturbing events later in the novel.

One of these opportunities is seen in Chapter 10 when the children are embarrassed by their father's lack of interest in 'manly' pursuits. Readers have a more rounded picture of Atticus than his children have, seeing him not only through the eyes of Calpurnia and Miss Maudie, but also appreciating those of his qualities the children do not yet value. The children's perspective is humorously limited. When Atticus 'proves' himself in the mad dog incident, they are baffled about his secretiveness. They want to know why he should have kept this wonderful talent to himself. Miss Maudie enlightens them and adds an important statement to the development of this theme in the novel: 'If your father's anything he's civilised in his heart . . . I think maybe he put his gun down when he realised that God had given him an unfair advantage over most living things.' The children are learning that skills and abilities are to be used to support a caring society, they are not simply to be a source of personal pride. Later, Atticus is to use his skills as a lawyer to defend Tom Robinson.

Another example follows closely. When Mrs Dubose insults Jem and Scout so vindictively Jem feels it deeply and takes his revenge. Atticus' reaction to this is to provide a further opportunity for advancing the children's moral education. He arranges things so that Jem will have the chance to come to understand Mrs Dubose better through close and continuous contact with her for a month. He hopes that during this time Jem will realise what she is and why she acts the way she does. This is a practical, concrete lesson which develops the discussion Atticus had with Scout about Miss Caroline and the Ewells. Jem learns to be polite, however insulting Mrs Dubose is, and we find he develops a new maturity, learning to control his feelings. Atticus eventually tells them how they have helped the old lady to die free of her morphine addiction and while Jem cannot accept just now that she is the bravest lady his father ever knew, the incident makes a great impression upon him and helps to prepare him for the experiences to come.

The theme of learning to understand other people, is most fully developed in the children's relationship with Boo Radley. At the beginning of the novel Boo is seen as a fantasy figure, a dangerous lunatic, almost a wild animal who stalks by night, while at its close he is recognised as their friend and neighbour. Throughout the novel this change in the children's understanding of him takes place in different ways and at different times. In Chapter 4 they begin their game 'One Man's Family' and enact a dramatic version of Boo's life based on gossip and rumour. Scout is rolled too near the house in a tyre and hears laughter. The real Boo and the fantasy Boo are both confronted, but are poles apart in the children's imagination. It is not until Jem has an intuition about the 'gifts' that any attempt to understand the real Boo is made. Miss Maudie relates his background to Scout but it does not seem to make any difference to the way she feels about him, as we see in Chapter 6 when the children make their night visit to the Radley house. In Chapter 7 Jem begins to understand something of Boo's real existence. He has already had qualms about the game 'One Man's Family' when Atticus disapproves of it, but it is not until he finds his trousers repaired that Boo's real character begins to fall into place. When Nathan Radley fills the tree hole, Jem realises what kind of life Boo is condemned to live and is so moved by this discovery that he weeps. He has begun to see things from Boo's point of view and to realise what it means to be Boo Radley, a complete contrast to the concept of him they enacted in their heartless game.

While Jem is maturing fast, emotionally and morally, Scout is left behind. She is unaware of the 'real' Boo until the close of the novel. She has had intimations, such as the time she asks Dill why Boo Radley does not run away, but even Dill shows a greater understanding in his reply. 'Maybe he doesn't have anywhere to run off to.' In Chapter 26, when Scout reviews their early relationship with Boo, we find that two years have effected a considerable change in her attitudes. She feels remorse, recognising that their childish pranks must have been 'sheer torment' for Boo, the words used themselves reinforcing the 'hell' image. When Scout stands on the Radley porch at the close of the novel and sees the street she knows so well from Boo's point of view (literally), this theme is brought to a brilliant conclusion.

## 3.4 WHAT IS MORAL COURAGE?

Understanding will not of itself remove evil from Maycomb society. Courage, too, is necessary, the kind of courage Atticus displays, determined to do what is right, no matter what the personal cost.

In Chapter 1 Dill describes his impression of fear in Maycomb. We find here that fear goes hand in hand with ignorance, and that prejudice and injustice are the result. But we also find many examples of courage: Chuck Little stands up to Burris Ewell, Scout insists on accompanying Jem to Mrs Dubose's creepy house, Miss Maudie stoically accepts the loss of her house by fire, Mr Avery puts himself at risk when he tries to rescue Miss Maudie's furniture, Atticus sits outside the county jail awaiting the lynch mob with only a newspaper for company, Mrs Dubose struggles to overcome her morphine addiction, Helen Robinson shows quiet fortitude after Tom's death, Mr Underwood risks losing subscribers when he condemns Tom's death in his newspaper, and frail Boo Radley is prepared to confront the drunken Bob Ewell. Other examples can be found which demonstrate different kinds of courage.

One of the most important themes of the novel is the distinction between traditional 'shot-gun' courage and what the author views as true courage. In Southern culture, great emphasis is placed on the type of courage typified by Nathan Radley, shooting at 'niggers' in his cabbage patch, the type of courage that scorns danger, is reckless, swashbuckling, and thrives on display. A fierce, aristocratic pride and this kind of courage are essential components of the Southern 'gentleman'. The shot-gun, we find, is much in evidence in Maycomb and the symbolism of the title suggests how inhumane such a culture can be. It is this kind of courage that Atticus is seen to lack when his children describe him as 'feeble' in Chapter 10. His lack of manliness, his lack of interest in fishing and hunting, in poker, smoking and drinking, all cause his children embarrassment when they compare him to their classmates' fathers. Atticus does not act like the traditional Southern gentleman and Jem is therefore delighted, after the shooting of the mad dog, to hear of his father's skill with a gun, proud of his father at last.

But Atticus takes the next available opportunity to present Jem with a new concept of courage. When Jem breaks down, receiving the white camellia from Mrs Dubose after her death, Atticus is quick to comfort him but he contradicts Jem's opinion of Mrs Dubose, telling his son that she was 'the bravest person I ever knew,' and continuing, 'I wanted you to see what real courage is, instead of getting the idea that courage is a man with a gun in his hand'. This is what Harper Lee considers to be true courage. A quiet perseverance that undertakes difficult and sometimes impossible tasks on a matter of principle. The kind of courage that does not burn itself out in a gesture, or dissipate under adversity, but steadfastly refuses to relinquish the struggle for what is right.

The position of the Mrs Dubose episode at the close of Part I obviously gives it great significance. As the latter part of the novel develops, we can see that this event sheds light on coming events, preparing us for a similar struggle in Atticus' defence of Tom Robinson. Here Atticus' moral courage is Tom's only hope.

It is the principle of justice Atticus is defending and this entails personal suffering. Atticus is also abused by the townspeople whose general opinion is given unrestrained voice in the invective of Mrs Dubose and the abuse of Cecil Jacobs. Both Mrs Dubose and Atticus are fighting losing battles but Atticus tells Scout that that is no reason to give up (Chapter 9). When he tells Scout to try fighting with her head rather than her fists, he is emphasising the kind of courage he not only admires most, but which will, in the end, prove most effective.

The hundred years he mentions takes us back to before the American Civil War (1861–5) when the South fought to preserve slavery against the liberal North, who fought to abolish it. The North won, but despite this, maybe even because of it, Southern attitudes hardened and the negroes were free in name only. Some of the early, fanciful descriptions of Boo Radley echo documented descriptions of negroes by Southern women; accounts as fanciful as Miss Stephanie Crawford's and as lurid as Jem's, can be found. Against this long tradition of racial prejudice, Atticus fights for equality before the law . . . fights and loses. But not quite. As Miss Maudie points out, he brings Maycomb one step nearer a humane society despite the personal tragedy of Tom Robinson.

The author is suggesting that what the South needs is more men prepared to be courageous in the way Atticus is courageous, putting down their shot-guns and their prejudices to 'fight with their heads' for a rational society. She also sees a need for more parents who will bring up their children in the same enlightened way that Atticus attempts to bring up his, teaching them the true meaning of Christian life, educating them to be citizens of a better society.

## 3.5  CHILDHOOD AND MORAL ATTITUDES

Harper Lee obviously remembers her own childhood with affection for her portrayal of the world of childhood is marvellously done. She likes children and shows them in all their moods and inconsistencies; their language, games and relationships take vivid shape before our eyes. She also respects them, believing they hold a torch for the future, that their simplicity, their fairmindedness, their loyalty and their courage is instinctive. She suggests that children have a natural propensity for good which the process we call socialisation corrupts or obscures. But we must be careful not to accept this concept too uncritically. '*Maybe* we need a police force of children,' Atticus muses. There is good and bad in all races, he tells us later, and this must include children. We also have examples of unpleasant children in the novel and Scout, Jem and Dill are certainly not presented idealistically.

But we do find many occasions when the children's ideas, their instinctive sense of what is right and wrong, seem to be the clearer for being unhampered by the complications of being an adult in a particular society. Scout's behaviour to Mr Cunningham is an obvious example and so too is the exchange between her and her brother after the 'Current Affairs' lesson in Chapter 26. In her simplicity Scout asks Jem how he can reconcile his attitudes to Hitler and to people at home. This question infuriates Jem who has left behind the simple-minded clarity of childhood and is now ensnared in the no-man's land of adolescence, trying to come to terms with the contradictions the adult world is demonstrating. He cannot yet answer the question in adult terms, but he no longer views life so simply. This difficult stage in his development is carefully chronicled in the novel, with all its confusion and pain.

Dolphus Raymond, himself with endearingly child-like ways – like his 'game' of deceiving Maycomb people about the contents of his paper bag – feels the sadness of Dill's transitory grief. It is only children Mr Raymond can trust with his secret, simply because they *are* children, and will understand. The author seems to feel that the world awaits them with its corrupting influences, determined to bend them to its prejudices and blinker them into its predetermined way of seeing. But is this really the case? We must remember Mr Underwood's reference to Tom Robinson's death as 'the senseless slaughter of songbirds by hunters and children'.

When Atticus makes his remark about the police force, he over-emphasises a child's ability to lead and to judge fairly. His remark shows his great respect for his children, to whom he is determined to give as enlightened an education as possible. Most of his disagreements with his sister are on their account. His way of bringing them up is obviously appreciated by them as we see in Chapter 9 when Scout is smacked by Uncle Jack.

One of the most important points Harper Lee is emphasising, itself a platitude, is that children learn. What she is at pains to show us, however, is that they can just as easily learn how to be unjust, cruel and selfish as to be just, caring and sensitive. In the novel we see Scout and Jem learning hard lessons through a series of planned and unplanned events. Their moral education is compressed and forced upon them by the trial. Their father's one concern here is to prepare them for this so that they come through it without losing what is good in themselves, and without catching what is bad in Maycomb, 'Maycomb's usual disease'. We have been given enough examples of children in the novel to see that there is good and bad in them all, in different degrees, of course – but they tend to inherit their parents' prejudices. What the author makes a plea for is that children may grow up to see what is evil in the adult world, without losing what was best in them as children.

# 4  TECHNICAL FEATURES

## 4.1  STRUCTURE

*To Kill a Mockingbird* is a very firmly structured book and shows considerable artistry in its design. When considering its structure, or the way the novel is organised, there are three strands to look at. These are *narrative structure, thematic structure* and the *internal structure of individual chapters*. We need to consider the interaction of these three strands with devices such as comparison and contrast, repetition of phrase and gesture, imagery and symbolism. These last two are dealt with in separate sections but it is well to bear in mind their contribution to the thematic structure of the novel.

Written in retrospect, the novel spans two years in the life of Jem and Scout and covers the crucial years of Jem's development from a child into adolescence. The *narrative*, or plot, is structured round events, recollected by Scout, which culminate in Bob Ewell's attack on the children and Jem's injury. The novel opens with a reference to this injury, and when it closes we feel the satisfaction of having completed a cycle in the children's life.

The plot itself might seem to be rather loosely organised, some of the events forming what seem to be discursions from the main story, but careful reading soon shows us what is happening. Every incident is built into what we can call the thematic structure which develops along with the plot. It is here that the *themes* and *issues* of the novel are developing. For example, while we will find the building of the snowman and the fire at Miss Maudie's (Chapter 8) good reading in their own right, we find a lull in the narrative. But important ideas are lurking beneath the surface. Fire and ice are elemental things and are opposites. Contrasts are an important element in the novel and Jem too is at a crucial point in his development, on the pivot between childhood and adulthood. Snow is a new concept for Scout, but Jem is able to deal with it: 'I'll never worry about what'll become of you son, you'll always have an idea,' Atticus tells him. Miss Maudie's fire totally destroys her house, but she does not repine, she lets it go: 'Always wanted a smaller house, Jem Finch. Gives me more yard. Just think, I'll have more room for my azaleas now!' Jem has outgrown his childhood and needs room for growth too, but he must suffer the destruction of his illusions before he can build the new world he will inhabit, a task his ingenuity with the snowman suggests he will be able to master. The chapter contributes important ideas to the thematic structure.

The novel is broadly organised into two parts. Part I depicts the world of childhood, with ominous rumblings in the background, while Part II moves us into the adult world which Jem, especially, is approaching. These appear to be telling different stories. In Part I the children are involved with the unknown Boo Radley around whom they weave fantasies and invent the game called 'One Man's Family', but in Part II the story of Tom Robinson is being told. However, we soon come to realise that here too the adults are playing their version of the same game. They too weave fantasies about people and hold irrational points of view. The children's game might have been torment for Boo, but the adult game leads to the death of Tom. Jem is prepared for the real world through the dramatic play of his childhood. Tom Robinson is no more a fellow human being to the inhabitants of Maycomb than Boo was to the children in Part I of the novel. The people of Maycomb do not try to get to know the real Tom Robinsom any more than Jem and Scout take heed of what their father or Miss Maudie tells them about the real Boo Radley. They each prefer their prejudices. When Jem finally does discover what kind of person Boo really is, and what kind of life he has to endure, he weeps for him. But few of Maycomb's inhabitants come to a similar understanding about Tom.

When Tom has to defend himself in court, he demonstrates that he is, in fact, a far finer human being than any of the jury who refuse to treat him like one (with the exception of a Cunningham, we discover later). Similarly, Boo Radley, who was viewed earlier as a lunatic, a freak or monster, finally emerges as a person of great kindness and physical courage. There is a pleasing symmetry in this further relationship between Tom and Boo, both the victims of misconceptions. Tom is imprisoned for a crime he did not commit, while Boo imprisons himself to escape a world which can do this kind of thing. We are reminded of Atticus's comment that there are many ways of making ghosts of people (Chapter 1). The structuring of the plot in this way relates the two men as victims and as opposite sides of the same coin. Their physical descriptions serve a similar purpose (see the commentary on Chapter 29). Tom's kindness to Mayella and Boo's kindness to the children help to relate them further and they are both seen as 'mockingbirds' who are able to understand others, as the mockingbird imitates the songs of other birds. Tom feels sorry for Mayella and is imprisoned because he goes to her aid. Boo leaves his voluntary imprisonment to assist Scout and Jem. This careful balancing, the one being very white and the other being very black, is satisfying to discover and contributes importantly to the design.

Chapters 10 and 11 demonstrate the way events are juxtaposed to make a moral point by contrast. In Chapter 10 we find Atticus surprising his children when he shoots the mad dog. In Chapter 11 we find that it is not this kind of courage that Atticus, or the author, admires, but the moral courage shown by Mrs Dubose; the kind of courage Atticus is going to need to defend Tom Robinson. A similar contrast is made in Chapters 12 and 13. In Chapter 12 the negroes are portrayed as a warm, close-knit community. Scout's language suggests this too when she refers to them as 'a solid mass of coloured people' on the pathway. In Chapter 13, however, Aunt Alexandra's ideas about families and 'Streaks' contrast strongly with this. In Chapter 12 it is the sense of community that is emphasised – what the people have in common – but in Chapter 13 it is people's differences which are stressed, what pushes them apart. This contrast helps to emphasise the author's ideas about society. A community which stresses in what way people are different, she is suggesting, is less likely to be humane than a community which concentrates on the ways people are the same. Calpurnia's attitudes in Chapter 12 reinforce this idea. She quite happily takes white children to a black church where they are made welcome, proclaiming with 'It's the same God, ain't it?' this essential tenet of Christian brotherhood.

A close look at individual chapters and the positioning of events for balance and contrast will make clear the careful design of the novel, and the author's narrative skill will be fully appreciated.

## 4.2 LANGUAGE

To Kill a Mockingbird presents us with many varieties of language. This diversity and range contribute a great deal to the pleasure of reading the novel. Within it we find the current slang of the children, Atticus' more formal way of speaking, his tendency occasionally to speak in a legalistic manner, Miss Maudie's crisp directness, the rambling sonorities of the Southern ladies, the negro speech of Calpurnia and Tom Robinson, the slovenly insolence of Burris Ewell and the offensive language of his father. Each variety has its own particular rhythm, pattern of sentence construction and vocabulary, which is acutely heard and faithfully represented. The author has a fine ear for language. We can also look at descriptive passages where detailed observation and precisely accurate expression produce a particular atmosphere. Atmosphere is finely created and sustained in the novel. We must also consider the problems of having a child narrator and discover how the author deals with the difficulties.

The novel begins some time distant from the events it describes which allows the author to use 'adult', or more sophisticated, language than a child of six, seven or eight years old could possibly use. Having a child narrator has many advantages (see the commentary on Chapter 1) but it does present quite a serious language problem which has to be circumvented. Generally, this novel manages it very well. If we look, for example, at the opening paragraphs we find not only a child's language but first, a mixture of reported children's speech which suggests their conversational tone and range of vocabulary; second, a direct statement which, while not using a child's vocabulary is what a child would observe and recount; third, a far more sophisticated use of language with extended sentence construction and an ironic tone. The adult voice can be heard in the presentation of Maycomb's history which is humorously ironic, yet the modulation to the child's voice and range of experience (see para. 8, Chapter 1), appears quite natural. This movement is skilfully managed throughout the novel and allows complexities of response, and points of view beyond a child's experience and powers of expression, to be conveyed to the reader. To see this technique at its very best, look carefully at the trial scenes and, especially, Atticus' summing up speech at the close of the trial.

The author is, however, a master of the language of children. Scout's racy, colloquial speech, the slang the children use, their faithfully reproduced conversations both with each other and with adults, make for lively reading and give the narrative an authenticity. Scout and Jem themselves have a feeling for language which can be seen in Chapter 7 where Jem is talking about Miss Maudie, and in the exchange between the children and Calpurnia about the difference between the languages she speaks among her own folk and with them (Chapter 12).

One of the ideas in the novel is that people learn, not by having something forced upon them by a rigid and outside influence, but by imitation, or example. Again, the mockingbird image suggests this: people will understand one another by speaking each other's 'language'.

Within the novel different sections of society are differentiated by the way they speak, and characters are portrayed through their own, personal variations. Language is important in characterisation and in establishing social status. We see how one section of society treats or regards another by the language used to talk or refer to members of that section. Scout says 'nigger-talk' to Calpurnia but just manages to stop herself from calling her friends and neighbours 'niggers'. She substitutes 'your folks' at the last minute, having learned, but nearly forgotten, that the term 'nigger' is offensive to black people (Chapter 12). A value-judgement is also evident in Scout and Jem's attitude to coloured-folks' talk, and Cal would be looked at askance if she spoke white-folks' talk with her own people. They too accept that language variations are closely tied to social status.

Characterisation through language demonstrates very well the author's fine ear, and a brief analysis of speech variations is rewarding. A contrast between speech styles also helps establish the themes of the novel. For example, when Scout has outraged Uncle Jack with her 'bathroom invective' and is trying to defend herself, their contrasting speech styles do more than contribute humour and authenticity to the exchange. Uncle Jack is objective and formal; Scout is indignantly colloquial. Her style suggests her intensity of feeling, while Uncle Jack's embodies his misunderstanding, his over-hasty assumption that Scout is in the wrong. This exchange contributes to the idea that understanding, and attention to each individual as a person with his own point of view, his own way of looking at things, is important. You cannot imitate the song of another bird until you have listened to it carefully first and this seems to be the criticism Scout is making of her Uncle Jack.

Burris Ewell's speech in Chapter 3 accurately forecasts the cocky arrogance of his father in the trial scene: 'Report and be damned to ye!' says Burris to Miss Caroline. His father uses the same offensive tone, and uses repetition in the same way too, bashing home his point. We see here that children assuredly do learn by imitation and example.

Mayella, too, is so unused to polite language that when Atticus refers to her courteously as 'ma'am' she furiously accuses him of mocking her and refuses to answer him. This leads Scout to consider the kind of life Mayella is condemned to lead, a life where no one ever speaks to her in the language of ordinary polite discourse. But Mayella cannot escape the characteristic offensiveness of her tribe. We hear, too, the characteristic repetition, hammering home her point (Chapter 18).

Tom Robinson's language at the trial also says a great deal about the kind of man he is. He speaks in the soft dialect of the negroes but, like Atticus, he treats Mayella chivalrously. He will not say she is lying, only that she is 'mistaken'. This shows his sensitivity. When asked to repeat what it was that Bob Ewell shouted through the window, he is unwilling to repeat it, considering it not fit for the ears of women and children. What a contrast this is to Bob Ewell's offensive tone and 'foul' expressions. Atticus has told Scout that one way of telling whether a witness was guilty or not was 'to listen rather than watch' (Chapter 19), and so authentic is the dialogue in the trial scenes that we, as readers, can apply this test ourselves.

Atticus' character is established by his use of language. Generally formal and courteous in speech – a style which often belies his kind heart and his sense of humour – he is straightforward and to the point in moments of crisis. Sometimes his language needs translation; sometimes his children understand him well enough, being familiar with his particular brand of humour, but need to translate for others as when Dill is discovered under Scout's bed. Despite the difficulty his language occasionally causes, Atticus has the gift of being able to express an abstract idea with a concrete image, making it immediately accessible.

The speech styles of all the characters should be looked at closely in this way. Look especially, too, at the language of Miss Maudie, noting how finely it portrays her crisp, but kindly, no-nonsense personality, and note as well how Dill's imagery conveys his sensitive and imaginative nature.

## 4.3 IMAGERY AND SYMBOLISM

Two of the features mentioned above are the author's fine powers of description and her ability to create and sustain atmosphere. Figurative language is important here and we find that the author is particularly fond of similes. Imagery appropriately conveys Scout's particular experience of people, place and event. Typical images, often of things to eat, can be found in Chapters 1, 2 and 6.

Character is established through imagery. The hard working hands of Calpurnia are described in Chapter 1, and we can almost feel the stinging slap she gives Scout who is rude to Walter Cunningham. The description of Bob Ewell in Chapter 17 precisely conveys his cockiness. Mayella's returning confidence and her underlying nervousness are conveyed by describing her as 'a steady-eyed cat with a twitchy tail'. Walter Cunningham's poverty and physical condition are evident in 'he looked as if he had been raised on fish food', while

Dill is described as 'a pocket Merlin'. The atmosphere of Mrs Dubose's house is conveyed by the 'oppressive odour' which makes Scout 'afraid, expectant, watchful', but her disgust of Mrs Dubose is conveyed through imagery: 'She was horrible. Her face was the colour of a dirty pillow-case, and the corners of her mouth glistened with wet, which inched like a glacier down the deep grooves enclosing her chin' (Chapter 12). But place, too, is conveyed through imagery as the comparison of the Ewell home to 'the playhouse of an insane child' admirably demonstrates (Chapter 17).

Dramatic tension is created with great narrative skill, Scout becoming our camera and conveying to us the precise details she is noticing herself (Chapter 10). It is with imagery, however, that the crisis is suggested through suspense and a feeling of unreality. This is evident again in the last of the trial scenes and connects the episode with that of the shooting of the mad dog. In both Scout is distanced from the action and the author uses the same imagery to convey to us that this is a characteristic response of Scout's to crises: it also links the episodes thematically.

The central image of the novel is, of course, the mockingbird of the title. At first the title seems to be just a cryptic half-statement, but soon it becomes evident that it is symbolic. Symbolism is a kind of sustained imagery where one thing does not simply suggest another, but is made to represent it. It is an associative device and can be seen working in different ways in the novel. The most obvious example is the association of Tom Robinson and Boo Radley as 'mockingbirds'. In the novel mockingbirds are a symbol of innocence and goodness, they do no harm, and it would be a sin to kill one, Atticus tells his children when they are given air-guns for Christmas. This is the first time Scout has heard her father refer to anything as a sin, and we are alerted. Miss Maudie's explanation illuminates the symbolic significance for us: 'they don't do one thing but sing their hearts out for us.' The mocker in the oak tree, as Jem and Scout pass the Radley lot in Chapter 28, represents Boo who could be said to sing his heart out for 'his children' when they need him. Scout realises the connection between Boo and the mockingbird when Mr Tate refuses to bring Boo before justice to defend his killing of Bob Ewell. He considers this would be a sin and Scout is quick to understand: 'It'd be sort of like shootin' a mockingbird, wouldn't it?' she tells her father.

Tom Robinson is also a mockingbird. It is to him that the title most specifically refers as in the novel we see him killed thoughtlessly and senselessly. Tom is innocent but is convicted, imprisoned and finally executed as he tries to escape. When Mr Underwood refers to this death as 'the senseless slaughter of songbirds by hunters and children',

Scout finally understands what has happened to Tom and why Atticus could not get a verdict of not-guilty returned. Atticus is 'civilised in his heart', but 'in the secret courts of men's hearts Atticus had no case'. The mockingbird imagery develops the theme of heartlessness and inhumanity in Maycomb society.

Atticus, too, is a mockingbird. His humanity encompasses all people and accepts their way of life as inviolable. He criticises his children for tormenting Mr Radley, telling them that people live their lives differently and have their own ideas about what to do. They must respect these differences, he insists. Atticus does not shoot, even though he is the best shot in Maycomb, because he thinks his skill with a gun gives him an unfair advantage over other people. It is for the benefit of others he wishes to use his talents. Atticus could be said to sing his heart out in defence of Tom Robinson, attempting to protect and nurture innocence and goodness. His neighbours, however, failing to understand Tom, sing only their own song, never the song of others.

Symbolism is evident in the novel in a less obvious way too. The closed shutters of the Radley house become symbolic of the Radley's attitudes, their closed minds, their lack of tolerance and charity. They also make a prison for Boo who lives out his shuttered existence behind them and in the shade of the oaks on the Radley lot. He is never in the 'sun' of friendship and neighbourliness, and eventually, comes to shun it deliberately, venturing out only at night. The shutters and the oaks figure in Boo's attempt to communicate with the children. When Scout is rolled near the Radley house in the tyre, she sees a shutter move and it is in the oak that they find Boo's presents. These details carry a significance beyond the level of the plot, suggesting that Boo is able to break through his family's imprisoning attitudes in his own, delicate way. When he does eventually come out it is under the shuttering darkness of night and this is prefigured by the solitary mocker in the Radley oak tree, singing out its heart in the darkness. By the close of the novel, the shutters and oaks, merely suggestive in the early chapters, have gained a symbolic significance.

The connotations of the word 'mocking' should also be considered. The trial is a mockery of justice, the missionary ladies' hypocrisy is a mockery of the Christianity they pretend, the children 'mock' or imitate Boo's life in their game 'One Man's Family', and Mayella accuses Atticus of 'mockin'' or making fun of her when she is in the witness box. A neat turn on these two shades of meaning is evident in Atticus' defeat of Jem in Chapter 5 where both the meaning of mocking in the sense of 'to make fun of', and mocking in the sense of 'to imitate', are understood.

Finally, the book demonstrates how, for many reasons, human values are mocked, and reminds us perhaps that God is not. Close reading will bring to the surface more and more layers to enrich this aspect of the novel.

## 4.4 CHARACTERISATION

The characters in the novel fall basically into groups, either of class or religion, and it is in the relationships between these groups that the author's message about the way people treat one another becomes clear. When Scout tells Jem that she thinks people are not so different as Aunt Alexandra seems to think, he contradicts her. Maycomb is a strictly structured society with a well-defined pecking order, and while one of the most attactive features of the novel is its presentation of lively individuals, we also find that social groups can be seen to have a function.

In each of these groups, however, we find an exception, a member of the group who is either in advance of his fellows where human values are concerned, or has the potential to be so. It is, of course, ironic that of the Ewell 'caste', it is Mayella who occupies this position. One of the Cunninghams makes a move forward for his group when he votes for a not-guilty verdict, Calpurnia is better educated than most negroes which makes her more articulate, Miss Maudie Atkinson puts the Maycomb ladies to shame, and Atticus is appointed by Judge Taylor to defend Tom Robinson because he is the only person who would really try to defend him.

There are also outsiders who belong to none of Maycomb's social groups but contribute much to the themes of the novel for this very reason. Dolphus Raymond has stepped completely outside Maycomb society by living with a negro woman and he illuminates their ignorance with: 'I try to give 'em a reason, you see . . . they could never, never understand that I live like I do because that's the way I want to live' (Chapter 20). Dill, too, is an outsider and this lonely, imaginative boy from Meridian illuminates Maycomb society's fear: he'd 'never seen such scary folks as the ones in Maycomb', he tells Scout and Jem (Chapter 1).

We find a truly Christian message in Atticus' reply to Scout in Chapter 26 when he says, 'It's not okay to hate anybody,' and we find the same principle at work in the author's delineation of character. While we divide them into those who are enlightened and those who are not, it is not the author's intention that we simply admire or criticise. None of them, with the exception of Bob Ewell perhaps, are portrayed as anything worse than 'mistaken in their minds'. Harper

Lee, through Atticus, extends to the characters of Maycomb the same chivalry that Tom Robinson extends to Mayella Ewell in court. It is their misconceptions, not their evil natures, that need to be reformed. The author's final message about 'Folks' seems to be Atticus' closing comment to Scout: 'Most people are [real nice] Scout, when you finally see them.' Even for the Ewells there is hope. When Atticus tells Scout that the Ewells can go to school any time they want to, it is not only formal schooling he is referring to.

*Atticus*, like Bob Ewell, has a namesake: Titus Pomponius Atticus (110–78 BC), friend and correspondent of Cicero. He refused to engage in politics but helped all prominent politicians in need. Atticus Finch is not concerned with the trappings of civilisation or the rigorous letter of the law. He is 'civilised in his heart' (Chapter 10). He stands for all Harper Lee admires in a father, a citizen, a lawyer, a Southern gentleman and a Christian. We find in his position nothing of compromise, but a wisdom and perspective that make him the conscience of his town, a position appreciated by Judge Taylor who appoints him as the only possible defence lawyer for Tom. Atticus embodies the humanitarian values the author wishes to present, the tolerance and understanding she sees as essential for life in a civilised society. He is an idealised character but this is no doubt because Scout admires her father so much and it is inevitable that she should present what is best in him.

His humanitarian principles are summed up in his statement that you cannot understand another person 'until you climb into his skin and walk around in it', which is the essence of Christian brotherhood and reminds us of God who was 'made man and dwelt among us'. At every possible opportunity, he demonstrates to his children how important this 'simple trick' is. Eventually Jem and Scout come to follow his example and learn from his precepts. They come to understand better not only their own father, but Mrs Dubose, Mayella Ewell and Boo Radley. These experiences, which form an important part of their moral education, prepare them to take their place in a world which needs more people like Atticus to lead the rest. Atticus' values extend into all aspects of his life. We see them at work in his treatment of his children, whom he allows to learn from their own experiences as far as possible, in his sympathetic treatment of Mayella Ewell and Mrs Dubose and even in the way he takes the trouble to put Walter Cunningham at ease when Jem and Scout bring him home for lunch. Her father has taught her it is 'a polite thing to talk to people about what they are interested in, not what you are interested in', and she puts this advice to good advantage when she meets Mr Cunningham with the lynch mob.

As a citizen Atticus is much respected and he has a highly developed sense of responsibility. He was elected unopposed to the state legislature and works to the best of his ability. Jem appreciates his father's position and comments that he spends his time doing things that wouldn't otherwise get done. Miss Maudie gets even closer to the heart of Atticus' sense of moral responsibility and the respect in which he is held by his fellow citizens in her reply to Aunt Alexandra's impassioned question:

'What else do they want from him, Maudie, what else?'

He is also a conscientious father. We are intended to contrast the way Mr Radley and Mr Ewell treat their children with the way Atticus treats his. He is honest and straightforward with them and they are secure in his love for he is always there when they need him. When Atticus sends Jem off to apologise to Mrs. Dubose (Chapter 11), Scout hates him for what seems to be his callous disregard for Jem's safety, but she soon ends up in her father's arms and gets the reassuring explanation she needs. At her most miserable, she always finds Atticus there. At the close of the novel this reassuring presence is made explicit as Atticus settles down for the night in Jem's room.

But not only does Scout feel that Atticus is there when she needs him, she feels that she is also indispensable to him, and Atticus' qualities as a father are contrasted with Dill's parents' deficiencies. Even when under pressure from the trial, and from his sister, Atticus does what he considers best for his children. He lets them learn from experience where possible, always ready with advice and support when they need it. His conversations with Uncle Jack in Chapter 9, and with Heck Tate in Chapter 30, make clear the way he feels as a father.

Atticus is also a Christian in the true sense of the word. His attitudes throw into relief the kind of Christianity that can condemn and execute an innocent man, and continue to support a society divided into a hierarchy of deprivation. His character illuminates not only the hypocrisy of Maycomb, but of all similar societies. Miss Maudie recognises Atticus as a truly religious man: 'We're so rarely called on to be Christians, but when we are, we've got men like Atticus to go for us,' she says, a statement which again suggests the Christ-like position of Atticus in the novel. Only through his own suffering can he hope to 'redeem' his town. This idea is reinforced by Aunt Alexandra's weary question to Miss Maudie in Chapter 24.

The trial of Tom Robinson, Atticus tells his children, is something that he cannot, in conscience, avoid. When Scout suggests that perhaps he is wrong and that most people seem to think so, he tells her that it is his own conscience he has to live with and this is not ruled by the views of the majority.

Atticus is also portrayed as the author's idea of the perfect Southern gentleman. He is courteous to all, treating the abusive Mrs Dubose with great politeness and patience and he raises his hat even to Helen Robinson's tiny daughter. We have already noted his treatment of Mayella in the witness box and his ability to put Walter Cunningham at ease when he comes to lunch. Scout pays a tribute to her father in this respect when, after a diplomatic move on Jem's part, she compares him favourably with his father (Chapter 28). His children are embarrassed by his seeming lack of 'manly' virtues but Atticus faces a mad dog and risks his life protecting Tom from the lynch mob, quietly and without fuss. It is also Atticus who rescues Miss Maudie's favourite chair from the fire.

Atticus' function in the novel is obvious. He is the model for Maycomb society – as parents, as citizens, as gentlemen and as Christians. As the circle of relationships and responsibilities widens, Atticus is seen to be equal to them all. If we find him a little too perfect we must remember his dry and ironic sense of humour and his great kindliness. He is not a paragon, but a lovable man whom we watch suffer for what he believes in. And behind his service to others lies a deep humility of spirit.

Within the white community, of which Atticus is the moral leader, we have found three distinct groups: the highest social class represented by the Finches and the Missionary Ladies, including Miss Maudie and Aunt Alexandra, the poor white farming class represented by the Cunninghams, and the feckless, parasitic type represented by the Ewells.

The *white ladies of Maycomb* are a distinct group which embodies and voices the narrow-minded attitudes and deeply felt prejudices which Atticus is struggling to overcome. Their conformity is humorously suggested by Scout's description of them at the meeting in Chapter 24, the ironic voice evident not only in her humour and the comic aspects of her blunders and misunderstandings, but also in the dry, sparse comments of Miss Maudie Atkinson. These highlight the hypocritical chatter led by Mrs Merriweather. These ladies wear their civilisation and their Christianity as an 'icing', or thin veneer, above their self-congratulatory attitudes and their callous disregard for human life. Their interest in the Mrunas and their treatment of the negroes at home amply demonstrates this. While the humorous presentation turns the tea-party into a kind of pantomime, the ladies are condemned out of their own mouths.

Their characters can be ironically summed up in Mrs Merriweather's criticism of Northern people whom she describes as hypocrites. Their complacency about their own position and the way the negroes are condemned to live, is evident in her further comment on the attitude of Southerners. Their treatment of the negroes has been turned into a virtue. Atticus' arrival with the news of Tom's death reinforces our awareness of this hypocrisy, for Tom has not been allowed to live at all. This short-sighted attitude is evident again when Scout reports a conversation between Miss Gates and Miss Stephanie Crawford after the trial.

A sharper picture of this type can be seen in *Aunt Alexandra* whose character is thrown into relief by Calpurnia and Miss Maudie Atkinson. She is quite different from her brother but appears to mean well and has the best intentions with regard to the children. She is misguided, rather than malicious and spiteful like Miss Stephanie Crawford and Mrs Dubose. She also has a real affection for Scout and Jem, so we do not condemn her outright as we do Mrs Merriweather or Miss Gates. But unlike Calpurnia and Miss Maudie, Aunt Alexandra is insensitive and unimaginative with very rigid and conventional standards. She is narrow-minded, puts labels on people and categorises them in such a way that their essential individuality is denied (Chapter 13). Her grandson Francis displays the same insensitivity and calls Atticus a 'nigger-lover', an attitude Aunt Alexandra appears to have outgrown by the close of the novel (Chapter 24).

It is Aunt Alexandra's inability to see when she is in the wrong that is her greatest fault. She admits her guilt when she sees it, as she does in Chapter 29, but she represents all the basic failings of the Maycomb ladies with her 'river-boat, boarding school manners.' She is not unkind but 'mistaken in her mind'. While she is not portrayed sympathetically, she is portrayed with considerable humour. Scout likens her to Mount Everest, 'throughout my early life, she was cold and there,' (Chapter 9).

When she arrives to take care of the children, her function is to highlight the rational and caring upbringing Atticus is giving his children, free from the prejudices that his sister brings with her and tries to enforce in his home. Atticus almost gives way on one occasion, but he constantly, and successfully, parries his sister's attempts to interfere with their liberal education and the way he is bringing them up.

We see this most clearly when he refuses to part with *Calpurnia*. 'We don't need her now,' Aunt Alexandra insists, but Atticus defends Calpurnia as an admirable mother-substitute. His ideas about upbringing are that it should be both rational and caring. To Scout, Calpurnia is a 'tyrannical presence' (Chapter 1). 'I seldom pleased her and she seldom rewarded me.' But Scout loves her and we see how well Calpurnia provides a secure, caring presence when Scout is miserable in Chapter 12 because Jem seems to be growing away from her.

Calpurnia's 'lights' are obvious when Walter Cunningham comes to lunch. Scout is sternly reprimanded for embarrassing her guest and even receives a stinging slap. Calpurnia's comment gets much closer to the heart of what it means to be truly civilised than all Aunt Alexandra's talk about Fine Folks. It springs from Calpurnia's natural sensitivity and perception, her ability to treat all human beings as equals, displaying the same kind of courtesy we have come to associate with Atticus. Calpurnia's values are not based on codes and conventions as Aunt Alexandra's are, but are human values. She is also full of common sense and is naturally diplomatic (Chapter 12). Calpurnia does respect learning, however, and has taught her son to read and write. Atticus' respect for her is obvious too when he turns to her for assistance in Chapter 24. She has the necessary qualities to help him inform Helen of Tom's death. When she leaves, Aunt Alexandra sits down in Calpurnia's chair where she is her equal, not her superior.

*Miss Maudie Atkinson* portrays another contrast to Aunt Alexandra and the conventional ladies of Maycomb. She is a friend and neighbour of the Finches and is characterised in as much depth as Aunt Alexandra with whom she is contrasted. 'A chameleon lady', she works in her garden in men's overalls during the day but sits on her porch in the evening in 'magisterial beauty', after her five o'clock bath. A chameleon, a creature which changes colour to blend with its environment, suggests affinities with the mockingbird who sings other birds' songs. We find that Miss Maudie, like no other white lady in the novel, has the gift of being able to step into other people's shoes and see things from their point of view. She is the sterling friend of Scout and Jem and one of her functions in the novel is to act as commentator, spotlighting for the children the significance of events, explaining for them what they do not understand. It is Miss Maudie who explains to Scout why it is a sin to kill a mockingbird, and who gives her information about Boo Radley, sensitive to the sadness of his life, aware of the secrets behind closed doors that make life miserable for so many. There is nothing secretive about Miss Maudie. She is as open as the outdoors where she spends so much of her time and her tolerance embraces all creation with one humorous exception. When she finds nut-grass in her garden, she attacks it with poison and fervour. This is analogous to her attacks on hypocrisy. Her 'acid' tongue is not only a contrast to the 'sweetness' which characterises many of the Maycomb ladies (suggested by the imagery Scout uses to describe them), but is as efficacious against hypocrisy as the poison she used in her garden was against the nut-grass. In Chapter 24 Scout describes the effect as 'blood-curdling'. Miss Maudie is portrayed as the opposite of what a conventional Maycomb lady should be in many respects, but this contrast enables us to see what 'sweetness' and conventionality really are in Maycomb terms: just an icing on the surface. The children not only love Miss Maudie, they repect her, 'Jem and I had considered faith in Miss Maudie . . . how so reasonable a creature could live in peril of everlasting torment was incomprehensible'.

Like Calpurnia, and in contrast to Aunt Alexandra, Miss Maudie is sensitive and perceptive. She also abhors religious bigotry recognising that a Bible in the hand of one man can do more damage than a whisky bottle in the hands of another. She has no time for people like the Radleys. It is Miss Maudie who points out to the children the qualities of their father. This refinement of feeling demonstrates Miss Maudie's position as a truly good woman who feels injustice as Atticus does, is sensitive to the sadness caused by intolerance and a lack of understanding, and is intolerant herself only of hypocrisy and cant.

In the novel Miss Maudie demonstrates the understanding and the courage (evident in her attitude to the destruction of her home and her willingness to say what she means) that overcome prejudice and fear. She is a truly enlightened lady whose influence, we feel, can only be to the advantage, not only of Scout and Jem to whose education she contributes so much, but also to the ladies of Maycomb who are put to shame by her unpretentious goodness and her willingness to speak out for what is right.

The *negro community* in the novel is obviously not realistically portrayed but is idealised. With the exception of Lula, they are all warm, caring, honest and upright people as far as we know, free from the hypocrisy and self-interest which characterises so much of the white community. Obviously this is not a realistic view and we are not intended to view Southern negroes absolutely in this light. In his summing up speech to the jury, Atticus refers to the 'evil assumption' that all negroes are immoral and contradicts it: 'some Negroes lie, some Negroes are immoral, some Negro men are not to be trusted around women – black or white. But this is a truth that applies to the human race and to no particular race of men.' In the novel we find no evidence of immoral negroes, nor even of those contradictions and inconsistencies we find in Mayella Ewell, Mr Walter Cunningham, or

Mr Underwood. Because of the 'evil assumption' referred to above, Harper Lee is anxious to portray the negroes in a positive way and gives us an unbalanced picture, but it is a picture with which we can sympathise because it arises out of her own intense sympathy with an abused section of society.

We are introduced to them in Chapter 12 when Calpurnia takes Jem and Scout to First Purchase Church. Here we find they are people who live out the proclamation 'God is Love' which is sewn on a silk banner in the church purchased by the first freed slaves. Even the cemetery is a happy one. They are portrayed as a united community which respects its leader. Reverend Sykes is able to keep them in church until enough money has been collected for Tom's family, suggesting that those without children make a further sacrifice. These people, poor themselves, look after one another in contrast to the way the white community officially looks after its poor (Chapter 19). There is also an intended contrast in the description of the Ewells' house and the negro cabins. The Ewells live in squalor while the negroes make the best of what they have. There is also wry humour in Bob Ewell's statement that the close proximity of the negro cabins is devaluing his property. This most deprived section of Maycomb society is portrayed as living in a civilised and Christian way, scraping a living from menial underpaid jobs, despite the deprivations and the lack of literacy and opportunity from which they have no chance of escaping.

The blacks perform the same function in the novel as Calpurnia performs in relation to Aunt Alexandra. They show up the hypocrisy of the whites. But in making this contrast, Harper Lee has failed to portray the blacks in a realistic way, presenting only what is best about them. This sympathetic portrayal is intended to intensify our feelings of outrage at the way they are treated, but this does not always work. Some readers find it irritating and accuse the author of the bias she is condemning in others. But as we read the novel we must bear in mind Atticus' statement that there is good and bad in all races. This point of view is forcefully made and is one of the novel's most important messages.

*Tom Robinson* is not as fully realised a character as Calpurnia. He is presented as a victim of injustice, a representative of his kind. He is the central figure in Part 2 of the novel and through him we come to an understanding of the negroes' position, especially at law. We can measure prevailing attitudes by the way other characters react to his situation and find especial aptness in the way the whites are unable to step into his (black) skin, or even view him as a fellow human being.

Tom's conviction presents a complete failure of humanity in the white community at large, and it is ironic that Tom is in this situation because he was able to perceive Mayella's loneliness and respond to it in a generous way. His character can be traced through the way he is spoken of in Chapter 12, and the little we know of him gradually builds into a picture that is coloured by his presence in the trial scenes. We find he is chivalrous, modest and honest as well as kindly, and we are deeply moved by his final despair when, unwilling to wait for an appeal by Atticus, he tries to escape and is shot. In the novel we find the negroes will have no 'chance' at all until more progress is made in the right direction by people as clear-sighted and courageous as Atticus Finch.

One of the ways in which this will come about, the author suggests, is through the education of the next generation. In *To Kill a Mockingbird* we travel with Scout and Jem as they make their difficult journey through childhood and we share with them the experiences which form their education and help shape their characters. When we leave Jem, nearly thirteen, at the close of the novel, we feel he is on the right road to maturity and we know that Scout, as the young woman who recounts these events, has obviously fulfilled her early promise. Her narrative not only demonstrates her lively imagination and her ability to capture people and place in a vivid and interesting way, but also demonstrates her understanding of other people, her warm humanity and compassion, and the sense of humour she has inherited from her father. The adult Scout is obviously Atticus' daughter. As Jem, too is seen to possess his father's qualities, the characterisation of the Finches is given an authenticity. They are obviously a family.

*Jem*, like Atticus, is seen through Scout's eyes. She obviously adores him. The importance of him in her life is obvious and the first and last sentences of the novel refer to him. He is a good elder brother to Scout, taking care of her, comforting her when she is upset, soothing her when she is angry and explaining to her things she doesn't understand. He occasionally has to put her in her place, and often asserts his masculine superiority and this leads to fights. While he patronises Scout, he protects her and knows how to handle her. We can see this especially in Chapters 14 and 23 when Scout has been upset by Aunt Alexandra.

Jem is a 'born hero' and initiates all their games and activities. He is clever and resourceful, which is demonstrated in Chapter 8 when he builds the snowman Atticus comments (Chapter 8). It is Jem who invents the game 'One Man's Family' and it is his inventive mind that describes Boo Radley in such a way that Dill becomes fascinated. It is also Jem who gets them out of trouble when they have been shot off Nathan Radley's cabbage patch and Jem has lost his trousers (Chapter 6).

Like his father, Jem is considerate and compassionate. We see both these qualities when he invites Walter Cunningham home to lunch and puts him completely at his ease by the time they arrive at the Finches' house. Scout pays tribute to him in this respect in Chapter 28 when she is embarrassed about missing her cue at the pageant: 'Jem was becoming almost as good as Atticus at making you feel right when things went wrong.'

His sensitivity to other living things is evident in the way he carefully removes the worms from the mud he is using to build the snowman, returning them to the back yard (Chapter 8) and when he tells Scout not to crush the roly-poly (Chapter 25). It is Jem who first realises who must have left them the gifts in the tree hole, and on realising what Boo's life must be like when Nathan Radley fills the hole with cement, he weeps for him. He has a flair for understanding people and situations, as his father has, and can enter imaginatively into their worlds. When he has the discussion with Scout about Fine Folks (Chapter 23) he is saddened by the way people treat one another: I think I'm beginning to understand why Boo Radley's stayed shut up in the house all this time . . . it's because he *wants* to stay inside.' Jem is disillusioned about the adult world he is entering and can't yet come to terms with it. After the 'guilty' verdict on Tom, he weeps with bewilderment unable to understand. It is Jem, too, who explains to Scout about 'mixed' children, recognising how sad their situation is because they belong to neither the white nor the black community.

Jem has a fine mind and intends to be a lawyer like his father. He has detailed discussions about the law with Atticus, but like him he also suffers. Atticus prepares him as best he can for the ordeal of the trial but Jem cannot come through unscathed – he is too like his father. As he leaves boyhood behind he develops the rational side of his mind as well as his compassion. At the beginning of the novel he knew *how* to make a turtle come out of its shell, but it took Dill to point out the cruelty of it. Jem respects his father highly and is loath to lose his respect. It is by emulating Atticus' fine example that Jem comes through. The characterisation of Jem is a fine example of the difficult and painful process of growing up.

*Scout* is as sensitive and intelligent as her brother. Her affectionate nature is obvious in her relationship with her father and with Calpurnia, but especially with Jem and Dill. Her empathy with her adored elder brother is seen on the night he returns to the Radley's house to retrieve his trousers, for Scout cannot sleep until he returns safely (Chapter 6). We are also humorously reminded of this concern when Atticus sends him off to apologise to Mrs Dubose and Scout fears for his life. Her loyal devotion is evident as she accompanies him on his punishment (Chapter 11). Her attachment to Dill is moving: 'with him, life was routine, without him, life was unbearable' (Chapter 12).

Scout has a sound instinct and many fine qualities, but she is hot-headed and impulsive, lacking the rational self-control which characterises Atticus and, eventually, Jem. Warm, friendly and open, her impulsiveness is often an asset, as it is when she is pleasant to Mr Cunningham following her father's advice that you should make people feel at home. But she jumps into fights just as easily – with Walter Cunningham, Cecil Jacobs and Francis. Atticus tries to teach her to 'fight with her head', referring to it as 'a good one, even if it does resist learning' (Chapter 9).

The principles Scout has in common with her father – such as her egalitarianism and her sense of justice – are held on an emotional rather than a rational level. She is deeply upset when Aunt Alexandra calls Walter Cunningham 'trash' and refuses to let her visit Calpurnia's home, because she likes these people and is naturally unprejudiced. Her Aunt's ideas offend her natural sensibilities as well as her sense of justice. But she has not yet developed far enough to see the inconsistencies in her own attitudes. When Dill is upset at the way Mr Gilmer is treating Tom, sneering at him, Scout is quite cool, accepting Mr Gilmer's treatment of him as something to be expected.

But as Scout develops she not only develops more self-control, she also develops a sensitive understanding of other people and the society in which she lives. This is seen as she comes to appreciate Calpurnia's character and realises she has a life apart from the Finches, and when she looks back in remorse at the way they have been tormenting Boo Radley. It is seen, too, in the way she is quick to understand Heck Tate's motives with regard to Boo at the close of the novel.

As a child Scout is precocious in some ways, never, for example, having known a time when she could not read. She has a very lively intelligence, however, even if she is rather resistant to formal learning and feels cheated by 'twelve years of unrelieved boredom' at school. But she is quick to learn from experience, especially when her feelings are engaged. We find she learns fast from the lessons Atticus makes available, following in his footsteps as she acquires tolerance and understanding to supplement her perceptive nature and fine intuition.

She is also naturally adventurous and rather a tomboy. She rushes into fights, wears overalls and resents it when Jem refers to her as a girl (Chapter 4). Mrs Dubose also picks on this aspect of her character when she insults her (Chapter 11). Aunt Alexandra tries very hard to change Scout's ways but Scout resists her attempts, even wearing her 'britches' under her dress when she assists Cal at the Missionary tea. But although she holds out against the feminine role, eventually she begins to adjust. Watching Cal at work in the kitchen, she realises, 'there was some skill involved in being a girl', and when Atticus brings the news of Tom's death she admires her aunt's self-control and presence of mind, and she emulates her (Chapter 24).

By the close of the novel we find Scout accepting her future role as a woman. When she is older and tells her story, she is able to look back at the young Scout with humour and understanding, recognising how the quality of her family life and her liberal upbringing have formed her character. In the portrayal of Scout's character the author embodies her optimism for the future of society through the education of its children.

# 5  SPECIMEN PASSAGE AND COMMENTARY

## 5.1  SPECIMEN PASSAGE

The passage chosen for discussion is the opening of Chapter 28.

## 5.2  COMMENTARY

This passage begins the chapter in which Jem and Scout are attacked by Bob Ewell and this opening prepares the way both in terms of plot development and in the building up of atmosphere.

We learn at once that the night is warm for the time of year, important when we find later that Scout falls asleep inside her stuffy costume, missing her cue and providing the reason for the children's departure after the others have left, refusing offers of lifts to avoid embarrassment. This also gives Scout the excuse to leave in her costume – important to the plot as it is the fat streaks painted with luminous paint that enable Bob Ewell to follow the children on this darkest of nights when the moon is down. If the night had not been so warm and so dark, if Jem and Scout had not left after all the others, Scout still in her costume, Bob Ewell would not have been able to attack the children so successfully in the way that he did.

The reference to Scout's trip on a root not only adds a realistic and down-to-earth detail, returning us to the children's journey after the lyrical passage which precedes it, but paves the way too for the difficulty of walking in the dark, even without the encumbrance of the costume which Scout wears home. Here Jem gallantly carries Scout's costume, dropping it in the dust when he tries to help her, an action which surely prefigures his own drop into the dust later when he is trying to protect Scout herself, in difficulties because she is wearing it. Had she not been wearing her costume both of them might have made a successful run for it, evading their attacker.

The big oak that they pass under – a cool spot – is a tree far enough away from the school and from neighbouring houses to provide a private place where children meet to play forbidden games, or to fight. It is under this tree that the attack takes place. Scout is aware of this as she 'felt the sand go cold' under her feet. So even the location of the attack is prefigured in this early part of the chapter. We find that Bob Ewell is able to take advantage of all the circumstances detailed here. This section prepares us for the attack by providing, quite naturally, a favourable set of circumstances for the attacker.

The warmth and the darkness described in paragraph 1 also contribute to the atmosphere and we find the tension of a thundery evening building up in a masterly way until broken by the attack under the oak tree. It is more than just warm, with the wind gaining strength and Jem thinking it might rain before they return home. But it is not the weather that will break. An ominous, oppressive atmosphere has been created in a few deft strokes as the children set out and we sense that something is going to happen, this feeling later being dispelled by the device having Cecil Jacobs jump out on the children, itself a prefiguring of Bob Ewell's attack.

The uneasy atmosphere is built up also in Jem's recollection of childhood superstitions and the rhyme-charm which keeps them at bay. This reference gives a pause in the narrative and presents a perspective by reminding us how long ago those times were, how much has happened in between, thus giving us the opportunity to look back. This is an important device as the ironic structure of this chapter depends upon our being able to do so, this pause presenting a pivot in the story of Boo Radley and his relationship to the children. This dismissal of superstition also lulls us into a false state of security, where Jem is concerned at least, for Scout is not quite so sure. Neither is she quite convinced about the harmlessness of Boo, but she finds the place scary just the same.

The references to superstition, to Scout's uneasiness about Boo, to the idea that a bird would not sing in a Radley tree, remind us of the legends about him, of the children's early fear of him and of his isolation. But here too is the greatest irony. Because Boo is not at the pageant with the townspeople, because the night is so dark and the place so isolated, it is he who hears the children's cry for help. Tonight Boo is 'bothered' as he never has been before, 'his children' need him. If he had not been at home he would not have heard them and come to their rescue, and it is because he is unlike the others in his habits that this was possible. Boo's isolation and his preference for the darkness now comes into its own, all of this being prefigured in the lyrical passage about the 'solitary mocker' which symbolises his sympathetic awareness and care of Jem and Scout, a reinforcement of the novel's theme of understanding and empathy. The Radleys were not curious, Scout comments ironically, but it is Boo who is watching and has been doing so for the past two years.

These early paragraphs prepare us, then, for what is to come and are a fine example of the author's narrative skill. The relationship between Scout and Jem is naturally presented while atmosphere is created within a realistic structure. In this early section of Chapter 28 the beginning and the end of the novel are recollected and pre-figured, and it suggests the turning point in the lives of Scout and Jem that the attack and the rescue by Boo turn out to be.

# 6  CRITICAL RECEPTION

*To Kill a Mockingbird* was first published in Philadelphia in 1960 to
considerable acclaim, winning three awards the following year: the
Pulitzer Prize – a most prestigious award won previously by writers
of such stature as William Faulkner, Ernest Hemingway and John
Steinbeck; the Alabama Literary Association Award; and the Brotherhood Award of the National Conference of Christians and Jews.
In 1962 it won the Bestsellers' paperback of the year award. It has
been reprinted many times, has been translated into many languages
and has sold millions of copies. In 1962 a film was made of the novel
starring Gregory Peck.

The novel was acclaimed by contemporary reviewers for its 'rare
excellence' and the way it presents the 'transient world of childhood';
for the tone which suggests it as a 'truthful story'and for its 'most
authentic humour'. Harper Lee is seen to have taken a recurrent
theme in Southern literature, to have taken risks and 'emerged
triumphant'. *The Times Literary Supplement* (28 October 1960) had
this to say about it:

> *To Kill a Mockingbird* comes from America laden with well
> deserved praise . . . Miss Lee excels in recapturing her childhood,
> and the children she writes about are worth knowing. Scout,
> brother Jem and their out-of-town friend Dill, are tough, imaginat-
> ive and well-informed. It becomes apparent that the Finch family
> form an oasis of enlightenment in a district rampant with all the old
> Southern vices. These come to a head when a negro is accused of
> raping a white girl. Scout's father undertakes the defence, and the
> novel thereafter runs the way of its many predecessors. But the
> plot is well constructed, the tone of the opening preserved to the
> end and the message one that can stand repetition.

Malcolm Bradbury in his review in *Punch* (26 October 1960) comments especially upon the moral themes of the novel:

> Harper Lee in her first novel has turned to a recurrent theme, the theme of the guilt felt by the white man for what he has done to the negro. She also chooses to tell her story through the eyes of children, a strategy I cannot normally bear because it prevents an adequate moral judgment on the fable. But Miss Lee has taken her risks and emerged triumphant. What is so good about *To Kill a Mockingbird* is not the substance but the tone with which it is treated. The story becomes a truthful tale about the difficulties of living well in a world where ignorance and prejudice make inroads on human decency. She understands her social scene, the American South; but her gallery of people has moral as well as social relevance. The good stand out from the bad at all levels. There is a splendid comic scene where the narrator, a young girl, goes to school for the first time and is taught by a Dewey-trained schoolteacher who spanks her because she is too intelligent and not one of The Group. But the point is made; intelligence and decency are positive values and this is why Miss Lee is such a good novelist.

Keith Waterhouse in his review in *New Statesman* (15 October 1960) notices the 'games' that are an important aspect in the novel:

> The innocent childhood game that tumbles into something adult and serious is a fairly common theme in fiction, but I have not for some time seen the idea used so forcefully as in *To Kill a Mockingbird*, a first novel by an American writer. The game is 'Making Boo Radley come out' which the children of a Southern lawyer play outside the old home of a family of foot-washing Baptists where, according to one among many legends, Boo Radley has been kept chained up for years and years for stabbing his father with the scissors. Pretty soon we are in the adult game, based on the same fear and fascination of the dark; the ugliness and violence of a negro's trial for rape and the town's opposition to the children's father for defending him. Miss Lee does well what so many American writers do appallingly: she paints a true and lively picture of life in an American small town and she gives freshness to a stock situation.

# REVISION QUESTIONS

1. What are the advantages and disadvantages of having a child narrator?

2. How is the theme of racial prejudice presented in a fresh and vivid way?

3. Do the idealised characters of Atticus and the negro community detract from the novel's importance as 'a truthful tale'?

4. How important is the theme of education in the novel?

5. How is religious bigotry treated in the novel?

6. Does the novel present only a Christian message, or are its themes universal?

7. Discuss symbolism in the novel.

8. 'In this country our courts are the great levellers.' Discuss this statement in relation to the trial of Tom Robinson.

9. *To Kill a Mockingbird* presents a variety of language. Discuss this variety.

10. How is family life presented in the novel and what is its function?

11. How authentically is childhood presented in the novel?

12. How does the novel present the way forward in social relationships?

13. What use does the author make of irony in the novel?

14. Discuss the 'hell people give other people without even thinking'.

15. How is courage presented in the novel?

# FURTHER READING

Mark Twain, *Pudd'nhead Wilson* (Penguin, 1969).
William Faulkner, *As I Lay Dying* (USA, 1930; Chatto & Windus, 1935, London). *Go Down Moses* (USA, 1942; Chatto & Windus, 1942, London).
Carson McCullers, *The Heart is a Lonely Hunter* (Cresset Press, 1943; Penguin Books, 1961 Harmondsworth). *The Member of the Wedding* (Penguin Books, 1962, Harmondsworth).
William Golding, *Lord of the Flies* (Faber & Faber, 1954, London).